GIRL UNDER
A RED MOON

紅月少女

GIRL UNDER A RED MOON

DA CHEN

SCHOLASTIC
FOCUS

NEW YORK

Some names have been changed to protect the privacy of individuals.

Library of Congress Cataloging-in-Publication Data

Names: Chen, Da, 1962- author.
Title: Girl under a red moon / by Da Chen.
Description: First edition. | New York : Scholastic Focus, 2019. | Summary: It is the late 1960s and there is no peace in the village of Yellow Stone for little Da and his family, who were former landowners; they are all persecuted by the Red Guard, particularly Da's oldest sister, Sisi, who tries hard to conform to the new political realities, but who cannot overcome the frightened hostility of the other villagers—so Sisi escapes to find work in a school in another town, taking Da with her, and trying to find a compromise between safety and justice, where she can make a decent life for both of them.
Identifiers: LCCN 2018053893 | ISBN 9781338263862
Subjects: LCSH: Chen, Da, 1962—Juvenile fiction. | Hong wei bing—Juvenile fiction. | Brothers and sisters—Juvenile fiction. | Families—China—Juvenile fiction. | Political persecution—China—Juvenile fiction. | China—History—Cultural Revolution, 1966-1976—Juvenile fiction. | CYAC: Chen, Da, 1962—Fiction. | Brothers and sisters—Fiction. | Family life—China—Fiction. | Political persecution—Fiction. | China—History—Cultural Revolution, 1966-1976—Fiction. | LCGFT: Autobiographical fiction. | Historical fiction.
Classification: LCC PZ7.C41815 Gi 2019 | DDC 813.6 [Fic]—dc23
LC record available at https://lccn.loc.gov/2018053893

10 9 8 7 6 5 4 3 2 1   19 20 21 22 23

Printed in the U.S.A. 23
First edition, September 2019

Book design by Abby Dening

To Lisa and Gie Liem for your beautiful grace

PROLOGUE

Grandpa had been a wealthy landowner in the small seaside village of Yellow Stone. His own father, my great-grandpa, had been one of the rare scholars to shine in the civil servant examination during the Ch'ing Dynasty, winning the title of *Ju Ren*, the equivalent rank to an earl. He was awarded the governorship of Putian County, a slice of paradise in the southeastern corner of China between the rugged Wuyi Mountains to the west and the Pacific Ocean to the east. Beneath it lay my tiny village, Yellow Stone.

The emperor also bestowed upon my great-grandpa

a lot of land that stretched as far as the eye could see. After Great-grandpa's assassination by a revolutionary rebel, Grandpa became a county sheriff and a civilian judge, adjudicating all villagers' land disputes, grand or petty, along the coast. Our family, the House of Chen, lived in Yellow Stone on the land granted to us by the emperor. We owned a chain of lucrative storefronts that were rented to merchants for a third of their profits, and our lands were leased to farmers for a third of their harvest.

Life was good until 1949, thirteen years before my birth, when Communism bled from Russia to China. Communism, especially in the form associated with Karl Marx, is the belief that private property is bad and making a profit is evil. Everything under the sun should be owned, instead, by the people. In China that turned out to be the top man, Chairman Mao, after he overthrew the ruling Nationalist government with his Red Army and introduced this radical, foreign idea to the masses.

Chairman Mao claimed he had liberated the great nation of China from a corrupt capitalist government, but the truth was less liberating and a lot more bloodthirsty.

The new Communist government confiscated farming land, factories, and stores from their original owners under the guise of land reform. They killed most of the landlords, including my granduncles, who were shot in the head, their gooey brains splashed all over the walls of their ancestral home.

Grandpa was one of the few lucky landlords to survive. They didn't kill him because he readily handed over all his deeds while on his knees, begging the Communist Red Army for his life. Though he was spared, what was left of his life was pathetic. They condemned him, sentencing him annually to labor reform. He spent over a decade digging hard soil in a mountainous region, building irrigation tunnels and making a reservoir.

When he became too old and feeble to work, the

commune party chief made his son, my baba, take over his labor reform duties. They believed the sins of a family were passed down in the blood and had to be cleansed for at least nine generations.

With the new Communist government, everything was turned upside down. Good was bad, and bad was glorious. For thousands of years, landlords had been kings, but now anyone owning even a tiny plot was condemned and sentenced to labor reform camp. Education had been as high and lofty as heaven, from which gold ingots sprouted. Now universities were thrown into chaos as education was condemned: It was a capitalistic enterprise, and teachers were the enabling bourgeoisie. Revered professors were locked up in jails; other teachers were sent to the remote countryside to be reeducated by poor farmers.

Everything was wrong. Nothing was right anymore, and wouldn't be until 1976 when the Cultural Revolution ended.

S isi awoke to Grandpa's hacking coughs from his bedchamber across the courtyard. It was still dark. The cold spring morning must have chilled Grandpa's lungs. He would want his hot tea soon.

She rolled out of her bed and lit a kerosene lantern. Hurriedly, she put on the set of matching blue jacket and trousers that Mama had stitched for her during last Spring Festival; they were her newest clothes. It was the Red Guards' Dedication Day at her middle school, and she had to wear her best clothing.

She gazed at herself in a narrow mirror and saw that her trousers had shrunk so that the bottoms barely reached her ankles. She tugged the waistband down a little and pulled the tops of her socks up, then scrutinized herself again. It would have to do, she decided, as Grandpa coughed violently. The sound of thick phlegm hitting the spittoon followed.

Lantern in hand, Sisi quickly entered the courtyard, where a pale moon gleamed behind the gentle arc of the roof and illuminated the paving stones, dewy from the sea breeze, and the courtyard well, sunken years ago by Grandpa.

She hung the lantern on an iron hook and tossed the tin can, tied to a rope, down the narrow mouth of the well and listened to it clink its way down to the bottom. She pulled on the rope and noted that the night tide had raised the water. The first draw of the day would be full and sweet, ideal for brewing Grandpa's tea.

Baba used to get up early to warm Grandpa's tea, but he had been sent away for another year of hard digging at Yellow Stone Labor Camp. With each political movement, which came now in surges, the commune cadres would arrest old regulars like Baba and send them away to dig irrigation ditches up in the mountains. Sisi had taken on the duty of rising early so Mama could stay in bed a bit longer. Mama toiled late into the night on her sewing machine, making clothes for her customers.

At thirteen, Sisi was the eldest. My brother, Jin, twelve, was next. Then came my sisters, Keke, eleven, and Huang Huang, ten. I, Da, was the youngest at eight. Due to the wide age gap, Sisi was thrust into a motherly role and often treated me like a young son instead of a little brother.

I shared a bedroom with Sisi, and the usual morning noises could be easily heard through the thin door she left ajar.

Sisi poured the cold water into a kettle and lit a bundle of rice straw, making a fire in the earthen stove. Grandpa's wooden door squeaked open, and in the dim light, his thin, shadowy figure shuffled toward her. His wooden sandals dragged along the cold stone, and his breath labored audibly. Ever since he had contracted a lung ailment, he'd been breathing like an old rusty saw. Frequent coughing spasms would leave him shaking like a windblown tree.

He mumbled his thanks as Sisi pulled out a bamboo stool for him. He sat, looking like an old sage, the light from the fire sparking a glint in his deep-set eyes and highlighting his sharp cheekbones and prominent nose ridge. He looked like a hungry caveman seeing day's first light.

Sisi lit his water pipe, and he puckered his lips and sucked hard and deep on his pipe, making the tobacco burn furiously with dancing little fizzles that brightened the semidarkness. He held the smoke inside his chest, letting it infiltrate and satiate every particle of his inner tissues before releasing it all out again like two tusks from his flaring nostrils with a glazed look of satisfaction, ready now for the chilly day.

The water boiled, shaking the kettle lid frantically with steam.

Sisi retrieved a folded wad of paper hidden behind a bundle of rice stalks next to her seat and pinched up a few leaves, dropping them inside his teapot. She poured the hot tea into his cup. Just as quickly, he re-poured the tea back into the teapot. Never the first brew, always the second one, he constantly said.

After a short wait, he filled his cup and drank it down swiftly in one gulp. He sighed with satisfaction and asked her to pour another cup for Grandma. Rising on shaky legs, he took the cup she filled and started shuffling back to his room, muttering something about Grandma's demonic cancer.

Sisi heard the door squeak closed, followed by Grandma's low groan and the protesting rustle of the dry rice-stalk mattress as Grandpa sat down next to her. There was the soft sound of slurping and the ensuing sigh of temporary relief.

Sisi started cooking rice porridge for the family. Placing the blackened wok on the stove, she filled it with water, then fed the earthen stove some more stalks. She scooped up the last cup of rice from the urn, washed it, and poured it into the wok. Mama would be worrying about the impending shortage; Sisi sighed as she fed another bundle of dried stalk into the fiery belly.

$\mathcal{S}$ isi quickly made her way to school, walking under the overlapping roofed sidewalk of the village's single brick-paved street. Some bricks had been stolen by villagers, no doubt to erect a garden fence or a wall around a manure hole. Each year, more potholes appeared and more bricks went missing, leaving the ground uneven so that it formed puddles or just became squishy mud on rainy days like this.

She pulled her straw-woven hat down lower in a futile effort to keep her blue jacket and matching trousers dry. The words of her teacher, Mr. Ma, played in her head again, about Dedication Day being a new birthday for one such as her. A new life to be given by her new mother, the benevolent Communist Party, so that Sisi's blackened identity could be erased and replaced by a brand-new one, bearing no linkage to her grandparents' sin of being bourgeois former landlords, the richest in the village.

The teacher's words gave sudden vigor to Sisi's stride as she passed the fishermen's store that sold belt fish coiled in wooden baskets and fresh oysters. She passed the butcher's store, noisy with the sound of striking cleavers, then she hastened across the stone bridge built during the prosperous reign of the last dynasty. It spanned the width of Dong Jing River, which ran down from the waist of the high mountains to the inevitable bosom of the sea that lay gleaming only a *li*—a third of a mile—away.

Docked flat-bottomed fishing boats and freight

boats swayed gently beneath the bridge along both banks of the river, resting for a night before journeying farther inland, carrying sacks of dried fish and octopuses. On their return trip, they would bring back dried mushrooms, smelly pine leaves, green olives pickled with salty little fish and shrimp to be gobbled down with rice, and neatly trimmed bamboo branches that would be used for building houses and furniture.

Some boatmen were still sleeping under their boats' bamboo-leaf roofs, waiting for their heads to sober and the morning tide to rise, while others were already cooking their breakfasts on little stoves called *han-nou* set on their sterns. A few pelicans swam playfully, morbidly dwarfing the flock of ducklings also sharing the calm water.

Both banks served as loading docks. Come early summer, during the *Duanwu* Dragon Boat Festival, children would jump off the banks into the deep river and swim with small bamboo baskets fastened to their waists as they dived down to catch slippery eels and search for hairy-legged river crabs hiding in muddy caves along the shallows of the river.

At the very top of a hill sat her school, grandly overlooking groves of budding persimmon trees and layers of rice paddies. At the back of the school was a high cliff facing the wind-choked bay, where legends of sunken boats and many drowned ghosts lived and were revived every year during the much-feared typhoon season.

Sisi ran up the quarter-*li* slope toward the arched entrance of the school, which was shaded beneath a thick canopy of old pine trees overgrown with long beards and dark leaves.

The doorman, Dar Gou, greeted her with his toothy smile and rocky limp.

Daughter of Teacher Chen, he always called her.

Baba had been a teacher at the middle school

years ago, before he was forced to vacate the position due to being the cursed son of a landlord. Before the new government, wealth and knowledge were respected; now they were dirt that stained you.

Dar Gou was illiterate, old, and old-fashioned. He admired the learned teachers here, giving praise to good students and scolding and chasing away the hooligans. His limp came from a bullet wound when he had fought in the Liberation Army that drove the Nationalists to the island of Taiwan, and he had been rewarded with the door guard job.

He inquired about Baba as he opened the door for Sisi.

"Baba is up in the mountains."

Dar Gou knew what that meant. Those he had respected the most had been sent up to the mountain labor camps to dig ditches, including the old principal, a legendary local educator. The world had turned into such a chaotic place. He said that this new political movement, the Cultural Revolution, sounded like a terrible idea. Why did they need to revolutionize such an old and good culture?

He spat in the dirt and wobbled back to his tiny windowed office.

Sisi loved school and served as class monitor, a coveted position among the students. Her two best friends were Li Jun, the dentist's daughter, a big-eyed and slender beauty, and Hin Ru, the pretty daughter of the village welder, who had four brothers who all looked alike.

The three of them sang and danced together as members of the commune's Mao Zedong Thoughts Propaganda Troupe, giving performances at all the many villages within the commune to celebrate harvests or important official holidays. Our government was organized like a layered cake: On top was the central government in Beijing; beneath that were the thirty-three provinces. Fujian was one of the most remote and forgotten provinces, and it had eighty-five communes. Yellow Stone was the largest commune, with more than two dozen production brigades within its jurisdiction, encompassing mountainous villages and seaside townlets. Though Yellow Stone was a little bird within the mammoth government structure, it was still a grand honor to be chosen as a member of the propaganda troupe, spreading Chairman Mao's gospel far and wide.

The middle school had been assigned a handsome new college graduate from the big Fujian Teachers University, Dr. Tang. Because of his advanced degree, he had been sent down to our village as part of the reeducation program, having been spared harsher treatment due to his influential father, an old cadre. He played the accordion with long and slender fingers, and sang with a silky baritone, even though he was an

English teacher with a PhD in English literature and not a music major. He practiced scales every morning on his gleaming instrument, filling the morning air with *oomph*ing alien musical notes from the window of his tiny apartment atop a flight of stairs in the quiet chemistry building. Sisi had once sung a solo with his accompaniment for a political rally in the school.

The empty classroom's windows had been blown open by the drizzling sea breeze, and the chairs were still on the desks. Sisi muttered a complaint under her breath about the sloppy half job done by yesterday's student cleaning team; they were supposed to put the chairs back down after they swept the floor, and there were still traces of white chalk on the blackboard. If he saw this, Mr. Ma, her political studies teacher, would be upset and spend the first half of his class preaching once again about the virtues of dedication to the Communist cause and about frugality and hard work. He would proclaim it the naked manifestation of bourgeois laziness.

She quickly closed the windows that were letting in a drizzle and put all the chairs down, lining them up neatly. Standing on a stool, she wiped the blackboard clean, even reaching the normally untouched smudgy corners. It was not until she had put away a fallen broom behind the door that she began to feel better.

Accordion music drifted through the closed shutters. This time, Dr. Tang was playing a popular revolutionary Tibetan song, "Beloved Chairman Is the Red Sun within Our Hearts." It was the same song she and her two friends had choreographed a lyrical dance number to for last year's National Day. They had worn colorful Tibetan costumes and twirled about on the stage, free and fluid. She smiled, deeply grateful that Buddha in his good grace had made this little heaven for a girl like her.

Her best friends, Li Jun and Hin Ru, arrived first, singing along with Dr. Tang's music. Without words, the three of them began dancing to the floating music, swaying to the exotic song sung by Tibetans living in the high Himalayas. When the song ended, they broke out into happy laughter and light chatter about Dr. Tang and his music and how they would all miss him when he returned to the city. Giggling, they started singing and dancing again. As long as they were together, songs would be sung and dances twirled, and life was good. It had always been that way with these girls.

Other classmates began to trickle in as the first toll of the bronze bell sounded, reaching the far corners of the village. The bell would toll again in five minutes, and a third time five minutes after that, at which point classes would begin.

When Mr. Ma appeared, his face was tight like a drum as he took some final puffs from his cigarette just outside the classroom. It was his customary ritual before entering the classroom, as if tobacco was his ammunition, something he needed to gain fighting strength for the day.

He was usually considered a friendly teacher, the kind who delighted in being among the young students and didn't automatically label you, but today he seemed quite different.

Mr. Ma was a prominent member of the Communist Party. He'd been an assistant army political commissar in the Eastern Division of Fujian Military District before being reassigned to his current mundane post as a village middle school political studies teacher.

Snuffing out his cigarette on the wall, he strode into the classroom.

Sisi crisply stood up and greeted him, which was her daily ritual as class monitor. "Good morning, Mr. Ma."

The rest of the forty students followed suit in a rather lackluster manner. This was the only middle school covering twenty square miles, and many students were tired after walking one or two hours down from distant mountainous villages.

Facing Chairman Mao's portrait, Sisi raised her right arm and saluted the great leader. "Beloved Chairman Mao, we wish you will live to be ten thousand years old with boundless good fortune." The class repeated Sisi's recitation mechanically.

"Sit down," Sisi instructed the class.

Chairs shuffled and squeaked as they did so.

Mr. Ma paced thoughtfully in front of the class, then began speaking about the shocking tale of some rebellious university students in Beijing. They dared boycott their classes and arrest Wang Guangmei, the wife of Liu Shaoqi, the beloved president of China, and put her on a public humiliation parade, condemning her.

This old news was only shocking to him, not his students, who were quiet, some half-asleep. They were mostly farmers' and fishermen's offspring. They would carry on their ancestors' trades, fishing the sea and farming the land. Beijing and high-minded university students were tiny birds in the sky, far away and passing fast.

But it was indeed big news. Even Baba had read me the news report and showed me the graphic photos on the front page of the *People's Daily* of screaming youngsters putting President Liu Shaoqi's wife on trial, calling Liu a flagrant Capitalist Roader—someone who had taken the road of Capitalism—and accusing him of plotting to overthrow the leadership of Chairman Mao, the supreme power, the reigning Communist Party leader.

What had caught my eye back then was the funny necklace the students had made of Ping-Pong balls and forced Wang Guangmei to wear to humiliate her for having worn a pearl necklace during their state trip to Indonesia. Genuine pearls. What a bourgeois act.

But the quiet in the classroom was quickly broken when a student shouted, "Down with Liu Shaoqi." It was Kar Min, a self-proclaimed Red Guard, who wore a red armband that was loose and at least two sizes too big for him, something handed down from his older brother and not yet officially earned.

Mr. Ma nodded in acknowledgment.

The other students still remained unstirred, as it was their nature not to be easily stirred. The people here minded only their own business, not the affairs of politics that turned easily this or that way in the blink of an eye. The sea and the land outlasted dynasties and revolutions.

No matter how hard Mr. Ma emphasized the importance of the swelling Cultural Revolution, his political studies class remained tepid, like lukewarm water.

But tepid wouldn't do. After all, he was the politics scholar on the campus. To heighten the zest in his class, he chose another way. He told them the Cultural Revolution was all about throwing out the old rules and replacing them with new ones. That was when the class truly awakened. Who didn't know about throwing old things out? Farming was all about the changing of the seasons and the growing cycle of new crops.

The class began chirping excitedly about throwing the old rules out, but the tide suddenly turned against Mr. Ma when a student named Crewcut, the school's tallest basketball player, called Mr. Ma an old and rotten bourgeois element who should be dragged out for a public humiliation parade and condemned.

No one knew what Crewcut was talking about. It was a ridiculous thing to suggest. But Crewcut seemed to know a lot about Mr. Ma's army background. He accused Mr. Ma of having an affair with the young wife of his army officer, making him a corrupt hypocrite, violating the virtues of Communism and Marxism that he lectured about.

A flicker of fear and embarrassment crossed Mr. Ma's stern face. He looked to Sisi, the class monitor, silently begging her to step in and help him save face.

A model student leader, Sisi stood up and ordered

Crewcut to apologize to the teacher. The entire class glared at the tall rebel as he swaggered up to the front of the classroom and bowed to Mr. Ma, who returned his own bow to the student.

Crewcut casually suggested caution on Mr. Ma's behalf. The army had sent a ranking officer to our region to calm down the potential riots, and it was none other than the man whose wife Mr. Ma had an affair with years back.

One heartbeat of silence passed, two ... then Crewcut sauntered back to his seat in the rear.

The class turned disastrous. It took Mr. Ma a while to regain his composure and continue discussing the nobility of Marxism and the eternal truth of Leninism.

The sky was pregnant with wet, dark clouds, frowning down on the earth with the face of a demon. Fat, slanting raindrops began pelting a new red banner hanging across the stage, proclaiming: *Yellow Stone Revolutionary Red Guard Swearing Ceremony.*

Sisi stood in the front Row of Honor with Li Jun and Hin Ru, outside in the muddy schoolyard where the entire school usually gathered to hear the newest political documents read aloud to them by the frog-eyed principal.

Sisi kept Li Jun's splendid long hair from being

ruined by the rain by sheltering her with her schoolbag, which Mr. Ma had instructed Sisi to bring. An unusual request, to be sure, but whatever Mr. Ma told her to do, Sisi did. He was the shepherd and she was his obedient lamb. Besides, he was recommending her as the new president of the students' Revolutionary Red Guards.

The naughty sun suddenly peeked out and smiled whimsically, and the rain stopped. The emerging bright sunlight made the wet ground dance with dazzling light.

Something special was going to occur. Sisi felt anticipation build inside her chest. It kept on expanding, making it hard for her to breathe. She had seen special things happen to worthy followers of the Communist cause before. It had happened to another girl without a shiny political background. She had been plucked from anonymity to attend the famous May Seventh Cadre School to study political science simply because of her brave act of writing and publishing an essay in the local newspaper condemning

Bin Xing, a famous Fujian novelist, as a bourgeois writer for glorifying lewd romance and faithless love between men and women. She declared Bin Xing's writing to be "a vomit." Such incendiary words had never been used before in literary criticism. It had garnered her notoriety and a spot in the college, grooming her for a brilliant future in politics.

The commune party chief finally approached in a motorcycle with an attached sidecar, a rare relic from World War II. He was the man of the town, with a fitting fancy ride. The driver sounded the horn, announcing their arrival with jarring force, the churning wheels splashing chunks of mud and rainwater with great fanfare.

The party chief was an olive-shaped man of middle age with a penchant for carrying a gun and shooting it off at whatever he saw fit. He had once shot a wild boar that dared venture into his bedroom; another time, he downed a seagull, a regal one, that had perched on the tip of the cliff, guarding the entire

village. He had been a bandit working the ranges of
Hin Hua Mountain, robbing rich and poor alike,
before joining forces with the Communist guerillas.
He could get away with anything and everything.

He sauntered to the center of the stage, preceded by
a prominent paunch. The domesticated years had been
good to him, allowing him to feast daily on his favorite
dish of well-simmered pork snouts and fatty jowls.

The chief was not just big but loud. In a roaring
voice, he announced the reason for his presence.
Cult-Rev had arrived. And he was here to bestow
upon the youngsters the honorable red bands. But he
didn't do much bestowing. He merely reached into
the box the principal was holding, grabbed a handful
of brand-new red bands, and threw them into the
crowd, causing an uproar among the boys and girls,
who started scrambling and fighting to get one.

The frenzy soon grew out of control.

The party chief fired a shot into the air, calming
the students down. Laughing wildly, he stepped

down from the stage and was helped into the sidecar of the motorcycle. The driver sounded the horn, declaring their departure as the old cycle grandly wound its way along the road, leaving behind three more unruly tracks in the mud.

Sisi had managed to snatch one red armband. It had fallen to the ground and was a bit damp and smudged with dirt, but it was new and smelling of the yellow ink just printed on the band that read: *Red Guard*.

I am officially guarding the socialist land under the red sun of Chairman Mao, she thought with pride.

The frustrated principal stepped forward, adjusted his glasses, and cleared his throat. He informed the students that he was going to read the names of those chosen. If a student's name was not called, they were to give back their red armband.

The list wasn't that long, fifty students in all. But from the mouth of the principal, each name was squeezed out slowly, with effort, like a goat discharging pebbly manure. The names of her friends, Li Jun and Hin Ru, were read off, along with other student leaders, but Sisi's name had not been uttered yet.

The last name on the list was finally read. It was not Sisi's name.

Her heart sank.

As the principal came down the steps toward Sisi, her heart rose again. He called out Sisi's name and, taking her hand, led her up onto the stage. With her standing beside him, he declared that they had been making a grave mistake for a long time—the mistake to put the daughter of a disgraced landlord in a position of leadership.

He snatched the red band from Sisi's trembling hands and ordered her to leave school and never to return again.

Sisi didn't know what to do or think. The words struck her like unexpected thunderbolts. Her heart climbed up into her throat and hot tears trickled down her cheeks.

The principal roughly shoved Sisi off the stage. The crowd was utterly silent as Sisi stumbled off the stage and fell. Picking herself up, she slowly began to run along the muddy road, following the three fresh tracks left behind by the chief's vehicle.

With tears blinding her, Sisi ran down the muddy dirt road, sunken with potholes and footprints of farmers and animals alike, some already swimming with tadpoles. Instead of taking the road home, she ran down the path to the cliff that overlooked the bay, slanting along the contour of the hill.

Her hat was yanked off by a headwind and flapped behind her, attached by a linen string pulling tautly against her neck.

Lamenting thoughts crossed her mind as she fled

the school. Why couldn't Grandpa have squandered all his money and land holdings on silk and satin, fine wine, bound-feet wives and concubines, on sedans and pleasure boats? Why hadn't Grandpa been a more ardent gambler and squandered all the family fortune and land holdings away, as had Ar-Jia, a distant aunt, who lost all at the gambling table right before the Red Army marched into our village? Her ill fortune turned out to be a blessing. Instead of being labeled a wretched landowner, she was a poor Communist farmer and suffered no residual consequences for having been rich and having owned a substantial part of the farming town.

Why hadn't Baba migrated to Taiwan as his only brother had done in the wake of their two-brother same-day wedding extravaganza? Her life would be so different now if he had.

As she neared the cliff, she came upon a flock of goats blocking her way, grazing on tender grass budding from the soil's crusty skin. Their shepherd was a shrunken old man called Jin Ju, which meant Golden Bamboo, a nickname given for his dark skin, tanned beyond recognition. He was a condemned man, a former Nationalist army officer. Sisi caught sight of him squatting under a thick pine tree, puffing on a smoke pipe.

She tried to push the goats out of her way, but they didn't even look up to acknowledge her folly. Only a baby goat glanced up at her and bleated forlornly as it was shoved aside by the grown-up goats. With tears in her eyes, Sisi picked up the baby goat and cuddled it to her chest. It struggled to get loose from her arms and bleated even more loudly.

Alarmed, Jin Ju, the shepherd, called her a thief and rose to give chase.

Sisi dropped the goat and again began pushing her way through the thick knot of goats. She only managed a few steps before tripping over a mother goat with swollen udders and long, sharp horns. Sisi fell facedown into the slimy mud.

Picking herself up, she burst into sobs. It all was too much, getting expelled, and now this.

She had been indoctrinated, purely and thoroughly, with revolutionary ideals, and believed in the Communist cause with all her heart and soul, even when that same cause claimed she and her family were rotten and evil because of their wealthy background. She had worked so hard to be a model student, to show that she could be a "revolutionary seed" despite her tainted background, and had risen above her circumstances to become the rare student leader. But now her family's tarnished background had caught up to her and dragged her promising future into the mud. Maybe they were right. Maybe she was indeed rotten to her bones, without any promise of redemption.

She turned east and shoved through the goats toward a side slope dotted at the very edge with tiny worship houses built by grieving families to house the spirits of those who had flung themselves off this cliff into the sea. Many brave widows had done so. Why couldn't she?

Be all. End all.

Sisi took a few more steps to the very edge of the slope. With her eyes closed and her arms stretched, she leaned forward into the precipitous drop, tilting toward the water far below.

She took flight, was beginning to feel free and weightless, when a bony hand grabbed hold of her heel.

Jin Ju screamed at Sisi, calling her mad as he pulled her back from the slippery edge of the cliff, gripping the ankle of her right leg with his calloused hand. He fortified his grip on her ankle with his other hand. With a final pull, he brought Sisi's muddy body back from the edge.

Exhausted, both Jin Ju and Sisi lay prone on the muddy slope, breathing heavily, the gusty sea frothing below them. Finally, Jin Ju stood up, pulling her up as well.

I sat on the stone steps leading from our back garden down to the slender river that ran in front of our house, keeping Mama company as she squatted on the lowest rung of flat stone and used it as a washboard.

The surface of the water licked at Mama's bare feet, the ripples making her toes look grotesquely huge. A tiny fish nipped at her toes and swam away. A baby turtle, barely an inch in diameter, paddled along the edge of the river. Tadpoles raced in the wake of the turtle, mistaking the turtle for their mother.

Mama was rubbing at the dirty stains of a shirt with rough brown soap made out of broken peanut shells because we couldn't afford real soap. Bubbles seeped into the river, smudging the purity of the water and causing a stir among the circling little fish, baby turtle, and hammer-headed tadpoles gathering around the enlarging ripples of soap bubbles. They opened and closed their little mouths, sucking in tiny bits of the nutty expulsion from the broken peanut shells.

I liked sitting by the river. This narrow belt of water that marked the boundary of our backyard was my little heaven. In the morning, I watched the sun rise above the distant mountain ranges and shed its brilliant light over misty fields of rice where cows plowed and mooed among the endless furrows of tilled land and farmers shouted to one another.

At night, I sat by the river and watched the moon swim in the depth of the river, unwet and unruffled by the ripples from my kicking toes.

Summer evenings, I laid small bamboo baskets filled with earthworms along the muddy edge of the river and pulled them up the following morning with a captured crab or two. Mama would boil them red into a soup flavored with lemongrass and ginger slices, and the whole family would feast on their briny flesh.

In wintertime, I would ride in a small wooden boat with Sisi and my other sisters, which they'd pole with long bamboo sticks around the bend of the river to nearby fava bean fields. We'd dock at a foggy cove, climb up a slippery riverbank, and wade into the bean furrows to pick ripe favas. Sisi would wait in the boat while we crawled between lines of beanstalks, picking finger-long pods and stuffing them into our coat pockets. Our fingers would freeze and our clothes become wet. After half an hour of picking, we'd run back to the boat and pole urgently away before the fava bean men arrived and caught us.

We would light the stove on the little boat, peel the beans into a pot, and wait for them to boil. The pungent aroma of the fresh beans would fill our nostrils and we'd pinch and grab up the boiled beans with our fingers and feed them into our hungry mouths. In short time, the beans would all be eaten and I'd drink up the sweet water we'd boiled the beans with, tasting like the scented soil they came from.

This was our port from whence we left the isolation of our house. This was where I dreamed on bleak winter days and reminisced on warm summer nights.

I dipped my fingers into the water, parting the calm surface of the river.

I asked Mama about Sisi getting promoted to lead the Red Guards in her school.

Mama replied that it may be too good an opportunity. A nail should not stand taller than other nails. Sooner or later, a hammer would hit it back, making it even with the others.

The wind carried a dark patch of cloud in from the sea. Fat drops of rain began beating the calm water relentlessly, like quick arrows plunging the entire depth of the river, reaching its bottom. The river water began to boil, bubbling like Mama's vegetable stew on our earthen stove, the mud at the bottom riled, making the water dark and dirty like the sky.

Mama grabbed the wooden bucket of clothes, took my arm, and we rushed up the stone steps.

Grandpa and Grandma sat at our rickety table, waiting to be served lunch. Grandpa was hacking and coughing up a storm, his throat disgorging the endless mucus he produced. I rushed into Grandma's lap, surprised to see her up, sitting at the table, rather than lying and moaning in pain.

She held me snugly in her soft arms and kissed my head. I basked in her grandmotherly scent of yellow chrysanthemum blossoms, which Mama oiled her hair with before securing it into a snug bun.

Grandma was surprised at seeing me not in school.

As Mama put away the clothes, set out chopsticks, and ladled out soupy yam for Grandma, she said my school was having a political rally, swearing in the members of little Revolutionary Red Guards. Teacher Han, our neighbor, had said that I should stay at home to avoid trouble.

Grandpa pounded the table suddenly, making the bowls jump, angry that his sins of having owned some farmlands had become his grandchildren's sins. He was always angry nowadays. The revolutionaries had taken his land, his storefronts, his manure holes. Now they were condemning his offspring, making even his littlest one a fugitive.

The shutters above our courtyard creaked as our neighbor Fan Yu began drawing them closed against the pelting rain. But at the sound of Grandpa's loud voice, she leaned out over the window ledge, trying to catch a phrase or two of Grandpa's angry outburst to report to the commune's political inspector. Fan Yu was a petite woman who had married the village carpenter, an even smaller man. On her wedding day, she had arrived as a naïve farm bride, mistakenly sitting on the lower foot stoop of the bridal sedan rather than seated on the higher and more comfortable chair. The whole town had laughed at her backwardness, except Mama, who had defended the bride newly arrived from a faraway mountain village, and chastised those making fun of her. But as time passed, Fan Yu had forgotten Mama's kindness and turned utterly hostile.

The last time Fan Yu had reported one of Grandpa's outbursts, it had been judged to be anti-communistic in nature by the commune's political inspector. Militiamen had tied his skinny arms behind his back and made him wear a heavy wooden board over his chest, inked with the word *Counterrevolutionary*. They had rushed him down the street in a humiliation parade where children had thrown rocks and wet mud at him and shouted, "Kill the Landlord," and, "Bury the rotten element alive!" He had fallen on his face several times, pushed too hard by a militiaman or disgusted bystanders. His face had been bruised and bloodied, and he had limped from a sprained ankle after being jostled by the crowd and hit behind the knees with sticks and bamboo poles.

Grandma shushed him. Pushing over the bowl of soupy yam Mama had placed before her, she told him to eat.

Mama placed another bowl before Grandma, and Grandma pushed it before me. She tousled my cropped hair, unevenly cut by Mama's blunt scissors to save money.

I smiled up at Grandma and readily fed a chunk of sweet yam into my hungry mouth.

Grandpa, prodded by my example, picked up his bamboo chopsticks and began to gobble down the food before him. A smile of contentment crossed his gaunt and wrinkled face as quickly as his sudden burst of anger a moment before.

In the little town of Yellow Stone, we had fore-warnings of bad tidings and precursors of good news. A flock of village boys and girls, some with runny noses, others with dirty feet, trailed behind Sisi, entering our house as if in a bride-welcoming cere-mony, except she was not dressed in red silk and satin bridal attire and there was no accompanying *yi-yi ya-ya* traditional band music.

Sisi burst into Grandpa's arms and sobbingly told us about the tragic events that had befallen her. Grandma said it was fine, school or no school. She only attended two years of school before war inter-rupted her schooling. She had done fine without it.

Surprisingly, Grandpa wasn't angry this time. He only asked for a drink of wine. Mama opened a chest containing his precious jar of wine. He sucked the drink down noisily, to the amusement of the village kids gathered in our crowded kitchen.

The children asked to be given some candy as a

small reward for bringing news and accompanying Sisi here. Mama said it was not Sisi's wedding day and there was no candy to give away. They only left after she promised to give them some when my sister got married.

There was a chill to the air in the semidarkness of dusk from early spring moisture. The village street had quieted and calmness settled over the household. The sun had set and dark night prevailed, restoring the land and sea, letting the earth repose.

Sisi poured boiled water for us in the nightly ritual of *xǐ jiǎo shuìjiào*—wash your feet, go to sleep. Five pairs of feet were immersed in the warm water of the wooden bucket. Our feet touched, our senses spoke to one another. Everyone was quiet, especially Sisi.

Huang Huang and Keke were too afraid to open

their mouths. Brother Jin only cared about some slingshot he had made from a tree branch that was taken away from him by a Red Guard leader who proclaimed that Jin should not be armed with such a plaything.

Usually foot washing was a noisy affair, with us pushing one another with our toes. Sometimes I'd deliberately smear my sisters' feet with my dirty soles, starting up a watery bucket battle, but not tonight.

As we dried our feet and were readying for sleep, there came an urgent knocking at our door. It was Jin Ju, the goat keeper, come down the cliff for a rare town visit. Without uttering the usual greeting of "Have you eaten your supper," he started scolding Mama for having raised a child who had done what Sisi did that morning—tried to jump off his cliff.

Mama was quiet, not knowing how to respond to the crusty old man, and kept bowing in apology. She offered him tea to appease him, which he readily rejected. Then she scooped and filled a bowl of boiled yams for him, which he stared at lingeringly.

When Mama asked the wise man what she should do with her oldest daughter, with Baba still locked up in the labor camp, he urged Sisi to run away. It was only a matter of time before they came to arrest her. Jin Ju gave Mama a piece of old paper with a name and address scribbled on it.

He said his brother taught at that school, and left, taking the yams begrudgingly.

At sunrise, Sisi stood by our door. A straw hat covered her head and she carried a small bag of rice, yams, and clothing. The day was young and she was road ready.

I pleaded to go with her.

Mama told me no. Sisi had to run away quickly. She had to find Jin Ju's brother before our commune's policemen captured her.

I threw myself into Sisi's arms and told her I could help carry her bags and keep watch. "I want to go," I pleaded.

She picked me up, held me tight in her warm arms, and told me to stay home. "I'll fetch you later," she promised.

Mama pulled me out of Sisi's arms, but I bargained for permission to walk my sister to the old pine tree. Permission was given.

Mama gave Sisi fifty fens in coin for the road and said not to worry about the money. She could always borrow some from her brother to buy some more moldy yams to feed the family.

We opened the door leading to our backyard, where guava trees, tea flowers, *gai lan* (Chinese broccoli), onions, and cilantro grew along narrow furrows of soil in the ruined plot of the former servants' quarters.

Sisi and I left our house in the secrecy of early morning calm, our old door of grandeur squeaking lightly.

The wooden bridge swayed willingly at the touch of our feet. Sisi held my hand. Baba said Grandpa had had the finest carpenter build the bridge with nanmu wood from the inner mountains, the kind that wouldn't rot during damp and moldy spring or fracture in the frigid months. It was composed of three planks pegged together and tied firmly with coils of wicker cane skin. Since it was all wood, with no iron clasps, links, or nails, the bridge made no hard noises, singing instead in soft rhythm with the sea wind and summer rain. Grandpa was a poet. He lived poetically whenever he could afford to.

The footpath wound among stretches of rice fields, its plants reaching my knees and scraping my skin. A few frogs leaped our way. One little one slapped its wet whitish belly against my cheek, tickling my face with its tiny toes and licking me with a quick flick of its tongue as if I were a giant worm.

I swiped it off my cheek, rubbing away the slime. I was used to slime. I played with green frogs all the time; they were my playmates. I caught them with soft baiting worms and had them swim like Olympians in a wide wooden bucket to see which ones were champions. I fed them little green worms that crawled over Grandpa's tobacco plants and lined them up on the lowest rung of our wooden stairs going up to our attic bedroom, where Mama prayed first thing in the morning, last thing at night, and many more times in between. She prayed so much that it seemed as much a part of her as breathing and living. She often forgot to eat, but never to pray.

After the daily race, I would bring the frogs back to the river and let them swim away to their nests among cracks in the rice fields.

As we neared the old pine in the village square, the village stirred with the overtures of morning movements, the sounds and fury of everything. Of life itself.

We could hear mother pigs being slaughtered at the commune's pig yard. At the pig market, squealing three-month-old piglets in bamboo buckets were being carried in to be sold.

Fresh steamed fish, octopuses, sardines, skates,

and mackerels on open bamboo steamer-trays were being sold by fishermen's wives along the little, narrow lanes of our village. Salted and tender shrimp stringed with reef leaf added to the color and aroma. The Lius were steaming their fine pork belly buns. The Changs were simmering their soybean pulp into a thickly nourishing treat called tofu blossom, which we drizzled with ginger sugar juice and slurped from porcelain dishes.

As we neared the Dong Jing River, the main tributary coming from the rocks and veins of the high mountains, villagers began appearing, tiny on the gray landscape of the seaside morning village, their voices just audible. They came and went like puppet show actors, staging themselves, moving along the journey of their life.

Men and women and boys and girls all around us were performing the Yellow Stone ritual of stumbling out of bed and dumping the contents of their night pots into manure holes, which were simply holes dug into the soil and layered with two slabs of rock for them to squat on. Only a short circular wall shielded them from onlookers throughout the day. The human waste stayed here until it was fetched up periodically with a wooden scoop and carried in buckets to spread over family vegetable plots as fertilizer.

Boys followed their fathers like butterfly shadows, here and there, carrying their smaller night pots, aimed toward the same destination. When the bottoms of the night pots were roughly scraped with pieces of rocks, off they went to the Dong Jing River, where they met up with their mothers and sisters to clean their pots with running water. Whereas boys and men swished and sloshed their bucket clean, females washed their red-hued sitting buckets by brushing them vehemently with a bamboo brush.

As we passed, a married woman looked up from the river where she was beating her pants with a round wooden stick and said to her companion, "Look, it's Sisi of Chen's clan."

"The one who leaped?" asked her companion.

Sisi kept her gaze downcast and picked up the pace. They whispered some more, then fell into sudden silence as we neared. I glared at them as we passed.

Farther upriver were Sisi's close friends, squatting by the rising water, washing their buckets. Li Jun, the dentist's daughter, looked up from her task at hand and nudged her friend, Hin Ru, who followed her gaze.

Sisi stole a glance at them and walked on. They didn't greet her as they usually did. Sisi had to pretend they weren't friends anymore because she didn't want to drag them down with her, and they had to do the same, drawing a clear line of demarcation between themselves and Sisi, or their parents could be smeared with a rotten political label. Li Jun's father had already been condemned a few times, having been called a counterrevolutionary dentist for deploying scientific medicine in his trade. Science was bad now. Hin Ru's father had also once been publicly humiliated as an "Authority Welder" because he had learned his trade from the red-haired, blue-eyed American missionaries who had once been stationed in Yellow Stone. Children of the condemned knew their places, and they had to do what was necessary to survive.

Yesterday had changed things between the friends. Yesterday they sang together. Today, no songs were sung. They kept their eyes low and resumed their chores. The mother river flowed and washed away all dirt; that's what Yellow Stone folks knew.

The old pine tree was home to a colony of swallows. Thousands of the birds were stirring, awakened by the touch of the earth's light, each singing a different tune. It was a fascinating sight. The old pine draws you in. The old pine spits you out. She keeps the good and the virtuous. She shades the paupers and drunkards. Within her reach, one is her child. Without, one is astray, a motherless vagrant.

Vagrant we were now. And motherless we felt.

On a low branch sat Crewcut, the tall basketball player from Sisi's old school. He spat into his hands, applied his spit to his stubbly hair, then fished out a pack of Red Cloud cigarettes. He tossed one into the air and deftly caught it with his lips. His buddy lit a matchstick for him. Crewcut drew in a mouthful of smoke, then jumped off the branch. The two of them walked up to us.

"Running away?" Crewcut asked.

Sisi ignored him and continued walking, but the two of them blocked her way. I hid behind her, avoiding the eyes of the two wolves. Crewcut said he had been named the new president of the Yellow Stone Middle School Red Guards. It was his responsibility to take her back to the campus for a proper public humiliation.

Sisi tried to step around Crewcut, but he pushed her back with forceful palm shoves. Fear gripped me so much I felt the strong and sudden urge to pee. "I want to go home," I said, pressing my legs together and squatting, fighting against a need to cry. Sisi squatted beside me and told me to go urinate in the rice field and not to be afraid.

I rushed to the edge of the muddy field, dropped my pants, and let out an urgent stream of hot urine. The spray wet the tops of my pants, making me tear up.

Crewcut whispered into his buddy's ear, and they laughed sinisterly. His buddy stepped into a rice field, caught up a brown-skinned frog, then uprooted a piece of rice stem from the wet soil and expertly peeled away the layers of the stalk, leaving behind a stiff string. He moved toward me while Crewcut used his strong arms to keep Sisi away from me.

His buddy quickly stabbed one end of the rice stem through the mouth of the gulping frog, pushing the pointy end through the frog's throat and guts until it poked out through its rear. The frog was in dire pain, its eyes popping as it gagged and struggled, its webby feet kicking up a storm, but it was held tight in the firm, dirty-fingered hands of his nemesis.

Sisi pushed Crewcut's hands off her shoulders as his buddy's hand shot out and pinched me down there, my pants still around my knees. He fastened the other end of the fibrous inner rice stalk twice around and knotted it tight, making me cry out in fear and pain. Then he threw the frog, stringed to the other end of this rope, onto the ground. The moment the frog landed, it jumped and leaped away, pulling at my sensitive flesh. The frightened frog yanked at me this way and that, violently trying to free itself. I screamed in agony as the creature continued to jump and leap. I tried to break the tough stringy fibers attached to me, but Crewcut's buddy laughingly slapped my hands away. I cried out to my sister as I followed the frantic frog's lead.

I heard a thudding sound behind me from her direction and glanced back. Sisi had punched Crewcut's smug face. He didn't expect anyone would dare fight him, least of all a girl.

As I shuffled after the fleeing frog, my pants gathered at my knees, there was another thudding sound. I turned and saw Crewcut punching my sister's face. Once, twice, and a third time. Blood oozed instantly from her nose and mouth; her cries of pain were deep and sharp. He was hurting her badly.

I grabbed the peeled rice stem and pulled, desperately trying to break the tough fibers, but the young bully twisted my arms behind my back and tied my wrists together with another rice stem.

With my arms behind me, my wet pants fell down to my ankles. I tripped and fell into the muddy ground, tasting cow manure, which had been spread to fertilize the soil. My fall only intensified the frog's determination to flee, and who could blame the poor impaled creature?

I turned my face in the wet muck and saw Sisi faring no better. Her lips were puffy and bleeding as Crewcut continued to pummel her with his fist. As he drew his arm back to land another blow, Sisi threw herself at him like a maddened water buffalo, tackling him backward. Never having fought before, Sisi was nonetheless a sturdy girl, and nobody was going to mess with her.

Crewcut fell and hit his head against the edge of a knee-high stone Rice Goddess statue. Sisi went down with him, on top of him. Crawling off her stunned foe, she came to me. Crewcut's buddy was wary after witnessing Sisi's surprising strength. Cowardly, he backed away, then ran off.

Sisi twisted hard and broke the fibrous string, freeing the frog. She carefully untied the knot around my abraded skin. Pulling my pants up, she lifted me into her arms, carrying me. I stopped sobbing after a minute and lay my head limply on her shoulder.

What a horror it was that people could do such cruel things in the name of the Revolution.

"I'm taking you with me so nobody can hurt you anymore," Sisi said. "Li Jun will tell Mama." She walked on without looking back.

The dirt road to Bridge Town was covered with gleaming morning dew. Each wet pearl carried the whole earth within its full liquid moon and lay shimmering on a blade of grass. The pitted road showed deep ruts left behind by bicycle wheels. A three-wheeled bicycle came toward us, carrying heavy bales of dried pine needles and twigs from the inner mountains that would be sold for fuel. I could hear the rider's loud breathing in the morning tranquility as he pedaled past us but could barely see him behind the mounded bales.

Bridge Town lay twenty *li*s to the west of Yellow Stone on a series of rising hills bridging the gap between the fertile delta plains and the rising plateaus of the west, but that was not how it got its name. They said that once upon a time, the mountains here were farther away from the old sea and the land between was flat, stretching for thousands of *li*s. Then an earthquake shook the land so mightily that it contorted the sea coast into the zigzagging snake that it was today. In that rearrangement by God's hands, a rainbow touched the sea and the highest mountaintop and pinched the two entities closer together, squishing the flat land into wrinkled hills, making the rice fields rise slowly toward the sky. Various stone bridges were erected, connecting the broken, in-between hilly lands together. Thus the town of many bridges came to be known as Bridge Town, luckily so, and not Wrinkly Town.

These bridges adorned the town, shining like gems, reflecting the sun in the morning and gleaming demurely like angels under moonlight.

An old arch at the entrance to Bridge Town was crafted with faded ornate wood lettering that bore the words *Qiao Zhen*—Bridge Town. It had been plastered over with a huge red paper banner proclaiming its new name of *The 20th Production Brigade of Bridge Town Commune*. The rain had washed away part of the banner, leaving one end hanging limply from the ten-foot-high arch.

We stopped by a clear pond to wash our faces and feet and wipe the dirt off our clothes as best we could. Sisi took a long look at her own bruised reflection in the clarity of the spring water, then finger-combed her shoulder-length hair and mine as well. Taking me by the hand, she led me under the shrine-like archway.

We found Bridge Town Agricultural Middle and High School nestled against a hillside right after crossing the second wooden bridge. On the steps to the school was a middle-aged lady sweeping with a long broom. Her gestures were wide, swaying left and right, fitting the word *sweeping*, as she sang a lilting mountain song. I couldn't tell if it was the sweeping broom or the beauty of the tune that made the swept leaves dance on the ground.

Sisi greeted her and asked if there was a teacher named Jin Han here.

"Principal Jin?" the lady replied.

Sisi showed her Jin Ju's old paper scrap with his brother's name on it. That was introduction enough for her. She led the way up the terraced campus, empty without the shadows of busy students or the usual noise of youthful exuberance. We walked up steps covered lightly with green moss. Atop the stone steps was an office building with a thatched roof, red floor tiles, and a portrait of Chairman Mao hanging on the central back wall. The rotting wooden doors were thrown wide open, in full view of the valley. Right in the center was a wooden desk and some bamboo chairs. Sitting facing us was a thin man bent over his books. All we could see of him was a shock of white hair as he peered down at the pages. It must be Principal Jin.

He looked up and smiled, revealing a broad face aged with wrinkles, and stood, tall and lanky. He came around the desk, and the lady handed him the paper. Principal Jin glanced briefly at it and made his way toward us with an even bigger smile.

"From Yellow Stone, my hometown." The older man shook our hands.

Sisi told him the name of our father and passed him our gift of dried squid that our mother had given to us. His big hands eagerly untied the straw knots around the leaf wrappings. Pinching up a handful of the salty sea creatures, he stuffed it into his cavernous mouth and chewed strenuously like a horse, with lower jaw going sideways rather than up and down.

He sat us down and folded himself back into his chair, picking out some bits of dried squid from between his teeth before taking a big sip from his jar of tea. Baba was his old friend, he said. Anything we needed him to do, he would do.

Sisi told him the trouble she faced. He nodded understandingly and said we could stay there for as long as he remained the principal. We just needed to pay a twenty-yuan boarding and lodging fee for the school year and work on the farm without compensation.

The working part was fine. We all worked in the fields on weekends and during long winter and summer breaks—we had the calloused hands to show as proof—but the tuition was no easy bargain. Mama had only given us half a yuan. Sisi promised to pay more when Baba was released from the labor camp and was able to take on house-painting jobs. Principal Jin smiled easy agreement.

The last hurdle was me, a preteen lad, not fitting any grade of his farming school. The little guy was too big a problem for him to solve, so he told the broom lady to find me something to do to make myself useful.

Revolution or not, a good man was a good man,

and he had tossed us a rope of hope. Now we could live another day and sleep another night. If not forever, at least for now. *Now* was what we needed, though *forever* might be what we wanted.

Readily, we bowed deep in thanks to our savior and followed the broom lady out of the office.

11

The broom lady's name was Mrs. Lin. With a kind smile, she took us down the mossy steps and showed us the rest of the hilly farm. I followed Sisi, feeling giddy at our good fortune. Just this morning, we were chased and beaten, but now we seemed to have found our harbor. Sisi cast me a quick glance, and I noticed that her usual frown was gone. She was never without her frowning expression. Grandma said she had been born with it, the worrisome type in the litter that others could depend on.

Taking my hand, Sisi dragged me along, following

Mrs. Lin as she led us around a sizable lagoon lined with swaying willow trees and built with finger-like docks on the clearest body of water I had ever seen. A dozen sweeping fishing nets hung from the docks.

The lady said it was called Carp Lake. The fish were so fat and dumb that they jumped into the waiting nets, willingly sacrificing themselves for the county leaders to dine on.

Beyond the lake were picturesque rice paddies, terraced gracefully down from the mountaintops. She pointed out fields of leafy taros and yams that were bursting with greenery. The fields down in the valley below were vegetable farms.

We soon came to the barrack-like student and faculty dormitories. There were weeds growing in a clearing with bamboo poles holding up a netless basketball hoop, lonely and nearly collapsed. On the hills surrounding the school were grazing cattle, white sheep, black goats, roosters and hens, cows and stout pigs, all rambling over the terrain, mindful only of the sweet grass, wild blooms, and tasty berries upon which they grazed. They looked up occasionally, not in appreciation of the serene scenery wrapping them or the sweet dew dotting their faces, but to gaze at their brethren feeding freely and blissfully in nature's arms, unbothered by the passage of time or the impingement of petty affairs such as the ones we faced.

The students' quarters were old army barracks—simple huts made of thatched roofs, walled with bamboo poles and thick layers of dried bamboo leaves, and rafted together by strenuous palm threads. There were a dozen rows of them escalating upward along the rise of the clearing and up the surrounding slopes. Each hut had bamboo doors framed by staunch poles. The doors were unlatched and swung in the wind, adding squeaky notes to the calm of the valley.

Mrs. Lin pushed a door open to reveal a narrow, windowless space with a dirt floor and two bunk beds built of hard, aged bamboo cylinders, laid with bamboo-skin mattresses and hard half-cut bamboo segments that served as pillows. Mrs. Lin told Sisi she would share this room with a girl named Su Lan from the town of Jian Kou.

Sisi took the empty low bed. Stowing her bags, she bowed to thank Mrs. Lin.

"Now, you," Mrs. Lin said, taking my hand. Sisi and I followed her out onto a thatch-roof-covered walkway. My room was in the same row but all the way at the end. The doorframe was carved with the military code *No. 25*. Unlike the other doors left ajar, this door was latched.

It was a special room with a stove in it, Mrs. Lin explained, made for an army chief. She knocked on the door. "Open the door, Ya Ba." *Ya Ba* meant mute.

After a lull, the sound of quiet feet shuffling was heard. An iron latch inside was pulled, unlocking the door, and the feet shuffled back.

Mrs. Lin nudged the door open. I followed, my bag in hand, with Sisi behind me. The room was neat.

A desk stood in the center next to an earthen stove on which a pot of rice and pork was left uncovered and uneaten. Ya Ba sat on his bed, turned away from us, his longish hair draping over his shoulders. Mrs. Lin covered the pot with a lid and showed me to a little narrow wooden bed on the opposite wall where I would sleep. Ya Ba turned and took a quick peek at us before we left and closed the door behind us.

It was close to the noon meal. Mrs. Lin took us to the back of a large kitchen with the biggest vats and frying woks I'd ever seen, each simmering, boiling, steaming, or grilling something. A sweaty, fat cook was too busy even to notice us enter his domain. He sang as he lifted this pot or that wok and tossed in a dollop of this sauce and that spice, mixing them with a long wooden ladle.

A big snapping turtle was slowly crossing the dirt floor between us and the cook. The cook picked the large turtle up, threw it outside the kitchen, and resumed his work. The turtle landed on its feet, turned, and started slowly back toward the kitchen.

Mrs. Lin pushed open a door that led into an inner dining room with lacquered furniture and some watercolor paintings inscribed with the most fluid calligraphy poems hanging on the wall.

She threw us two cloth towels, told us to go outside to wash our hands and faces, and led us to a running spring. Bending over the cool water, I used the towel to scoop up some water and furiously wash my face, shoulders, arms, and chest.

"Don't forget your armpits. Splash them so you don't ruin their lunch with your monkey smell," Sisi said, smiling.

I leaned over, splashing cool water onto my sweaty pits, left and right, then up and down. Sisi dried my back and wiped my face, then patted her own face dry. She took a careful look at her watery reflection, scraping her bangs back over her temples to reveal her wholesome face.

We reentered the kitchen to find the cook trying to catch a fat carp that had just leaped out of a fishnet. He whacked the fish's head with a big cleaver. The fish stopped flopping and lay stunned on the dirt floor, limply gasping and twitching its long beards.

Mrs. Lin handed us two sets of red uniforms and told us to change.

Sisi put on a snug blouse with a *Military Use Only* label on her chest. I put mine on, a much smaller size, stitched with a different label of *Land Help*.

At noontime, a bronze bell tolled, the sound lingering in the valley. Tribes of young laborers were called back, looking tiny from afar, then getting bigger as they moved down the paths, flooding the basin. Hoes, spades, sickles, and bamboo manure baskets were carried over shoulders as, with a tired gait asunder, they swamped into the communal dining hall attached to the eastern end of the kitchen. Soon the sounds of chopsticks picking and bowls clicking pre-vailed as the young mouths chewed what bounty nature gave them, bounty that had been planted and harvested with their own hands from the surround-ing soil.

Separated by a curtained doorway was the principal's private dining room. He entered with the local Bridge Town mayor, another former bandit who joined the Communist Red Army. He was a stout man in his forties with a smiling monk's face and large Buddha ears. He wore a green army uni-form with four prominent pockets, a symbol of his former officer rank, not the two-pocketed low-rank variety. With a bemused expression, he gazed at Sisi, his eyes following her gestures as she unfolded the steamed towels and passed them to him and his host. He held the hot towel in his meaty hands absently, not looking away from Sisi until she bowed out of the room.

Back in the kitchen, I asked Sisi why the mayor

had stared at her like that. She blushed and just shook her head, saying I was too young to understand grown-up things.

Mrs. Lin overheard our conversation and asked if I liked to look at girls, the pretty ones.

I nodded shyly.

"See," she said. "It's the same thing. The mayor likes Sisi because she is young and healthy."

"But he's old," I replied.

Mrs. Lin smiled. "The older men get, the more they like to look at girls."

When Mrs. Lin left, I asked Sisi if the mayor made her uncomfortable.

She nodded and told me to shut up.

I said I didn't like it, having her looked at like that. Why did she have to put up with it?

Sisi said it was because the mayor was the leader of the town and he was supporting Principal Jin, and could help keep us safe here, away from the wolves of Yellow Stone.

—

My duty of the day was to serve a cleansing cup of oolong tea before the meal. I poured the tea from an iron kettle, but the mayor hardly noticed me, his eyes still staring at the moving curtains separating the room from the noisy kitchen.

The mayor and his host bickered like an old couple. The former complained about not being invited often enough. The latter told him to just eat, drink, and shut up. The mayor sipped at the tea and pulled a cigarette out of an open Shanghai-brand pack the principal had laid on the table. I lit it for him with a lighter, and his eyes moved to me, wondering who I was. But he wasn't in the least interested in me. He asked for Sisi's name and I told him. When I offered my name to him, his reply was: "Pour more tea."

I did so.

I heard Mrs. Lin calling me and retreated to the kitchen to fetch liquor.

Sisi brought out a plate of simmered pork knuckles, smelling of seasoned soy sauce, ginger, and fresh cilantro. I returned with a delicate bottle of Maotai liquor, a famous brand I'd only heard of and had never seen before, the kind that Grandpa often described as heavenly and sacred, the kind he could no longer afford and was only able to dream about from distant memory.

Sisi placed the succulent fatty young pork knuckles in front of the two men. Ignoring the savory delicacy, the mayor's eyes followed the movements of Sisi's hands as she carefully ladled a portion onto the guest's porcelain dish.

"What did she do?" the mayor asked Principal Jin, as if Sisi were not present.

Principal Jin ignored him, taking the time instead to evaluate my skill at pouring the precious liquor into delicate wine cups, a feat I managed without a wasted drip. Grandpa often praised me for my skill at the manly act of wine pouring. Even a drip beyond the brim and the drinking and joy of imbibing such was ruined. When the principal didn't scold me, I took it as mute approval.

The mayor persisted, asking again what Sisi was here for, his eyes tracing up Sisi's snug uniform, outlining the slenderness of her waist and her curvy figure. Once again, the principal ignored him. They clinked their cups and chewed the pork skin. The mayor mumbled on, in between his bites. He had just returned from an all-county conference in Putian. The county propaganda chief had read them mountains of documents, ordering lower cadres to toe the line and weed out the counterrevolutionary suspects and hidden enemies. Nothing he said interested the principal, who kept on smoking one cigarette after another.

We returned with five more dishes: steamed carp with its gaping head intact, eyeballs staring but not seeing, laced with ginger, onions, *gai lan*, and generous doses of star anise; a dish of fragrant pork belly with three layers of fatty meat; snow pea leaves lightly sautéed; kung pao chicken with oily fried peanuts; and a fatty duck stewed in hot clay pots. Mrs. Lin followed up these savory offerings with a huge bowl piled high with the whitest grains of rice I'd ever seen, making me ache with hunger pains. For a long time, it had always been yams and yams and more moldy yams that we ate at home. I couldn't blame my belly for having an internal rebellion at seeing the sumptuous meal on display.

The noon meal lasted for hours. Soon the room was infused with cigarette smoke. After the men left by another entrance, we cleaned up the table. Mrs. Lin wiped her hands on her apron and threw together two bowls of rice, topped with leftover food from the guest's plates. We chowed down every bit of it, licking up the last grain of rice and delicious sauce.

With our first chore successfully done, I saw quiet relief in Sisi's face. I could see the change in her movements, no longer rigid but fluid like a young flower tossing its petals in a breeze, opening itself up to the touch of a warm sun.

She took off her uniform and mine, hung them on hooks on the wall, and dragged me out of the heavenly kitchen.

*W*e left the kitchen to find the school had come alive with footfalls and echoing voices after a full morning of farm labor and a noon meal of rice and well-simmered pig snouts mixed with fermented soybean paste, and other unknowable scents of this part of the country.

Young gray water buffaloes, mother goats, slow-walking ducks, hens, roosters, turtles, and pigs milled around the students' ankles, enjoying one another's company. Farther up on the terraced hill stood a pack of wolf dogs, aloof with snouts in the wind, standing sentry for the school.

A pair of girls Sisi's age looked at us in passing. Another pair of boys, walking opposite, stopped in their tracks, glancing curiously first at Sisi and then me. Sisi lowered her eyes and pulled me along toward our rooms.

Pale city boys, I thought dismissively. They all had snotty noses.

When we neared Sisi's hut, an elegant girl rushed out to meet us, exuberantly crying out, "I'm Su Lan. You're Chen Sisi, my new roommate, Principal just told me." She grabbed Sisi's hands, shaking them furiously, leaning her slender frame into Sisi's full chest. Sisi returned her embrace, allowing two strange bodies to meet and their warmth merge.

When Sisi introduced me, Su Lan pulled herself away from Sisi's arms and took me into her own arms.

A sharp whistle was blown, lancing the air. It was

time to weed the rice paddies. In the straight sun, young bodies began hiking up the deliberate escalations to ancient green fields, delicately terraced and lushly nourished by rain above and rich earth below.

We climbed up to crescent terraces wrapping around the waist of the hill, each a half acre. Su Lan and Sisi tied on straw hats and draped towels over the backs of their necks. After tightening their waist strings and rolling up their pants, they stepped down from the raised margins into the muddy soil. Bubbles rushed up on their descent, as if happy for their coming. They knelt, reaching out their young arms, and began scraping their deft fingers along the columns and rows of rice stalks. They groped around the base of each stem and weeded out the roots of unwanted growth; had this not been done, the weeds would soon colonize the ground and the rice plants would wither.

They sang as they crawled along, side by side, in a fan-shaped fashion. Young rice stalks bent beneath their elbows, knowing they were being cared for, their blades gently scraping the girls' arms, hurting them not at all.

I found a spot along the margin under a stout banana tree, crawling with giant ants and lizards. I napped, waiting for the sun to set. It had only been half a day, but life had taken on a new leaf.

Hours later, I awoke in the dimming light, the amber sunset over my shoulder. It had been a dreamless nap. Ants were crawling over my feet, neck, and cheeks. I was confused as to where I lay. This felt different. There were chunks of animal manure around my neck and head and smeared all over my face. The light was pervasive, casting a curtain over the earth. The stout banana tree I had napped under was far away. The smells swirling around my nostrils were that of duck and chicken droppings, and pig feces, smells I knew well from our own backyard.

I lay there, looking above and around. In the distance, I heard the singing voices of Su Lan and Sisi. I raised my body up, the smeared manure that had been caked over me cracking. I saw Sisi and Su Lan step out of the rice paddy, hats off now, browned from the sun, their feet dragging as they walked along the margin of the field, strewn with pulled weed roots and useless leaves. They held hands, Su Lan leaning on Sisi, and Sisi's long arm over Su Lan's shoulder, looking like a pair of inseparable sisters already.

Catching sight of me, Su Lan ran toward me, anger darkening her eyes as she squatted and pulled me up. She knew who had played this wicked trick and vowed to address this injustice done to me.

Wetting her towel in the clear water of a nearby rice field, she washed my face, while Sisi took off my shirt and, scooping water with her hands, splashed it down my torso, front and back, to clean me. Su Lan rinsed her towel and carried me piggyback down the hill.

Soon I was laughing, affected by Su Lan's giggles and life force that seemed to well up from her back to my chest, warming my heart. Sisi followed us, picking up Su Lan's towel.

14

The following day, my other sisters, Huang Huang and Keke, came, saddled with two bags of dry, salted cuttlefish prepared by Mama as a gift to Principal Jin. They met us at Sisi's room.

Keke urged us to stay here. School hooligans were still searching for us in order to take Sisi for a public humiliation. We were not out of danger yet.

Sisi offered to feed them, but they looked to the sky, anxious to be on their way home. Before they went, Huang Huang pulled out a letter of gratitude from Baba to the principal, and a book for me, my textbook.

They left when the sun began its western descent, their slender legs and bare feet carrying them down to the plain, their thinning voices trailing behind them in sisterly chat.

*S*isi and Su Lan were serving the principal and his guests' evening meal. Alone, I walked down the slope toward the students' dining hall, noisy now with hungry students. It was dinnertime. The dim light of waning day filtered through the open windows of the rustic hall. Coarse smells rushed out of the kitchen windows, and pine-scented smoke funneled up in dark chunks out of four mighty chimneys.

All food was all good in hunger. My belly was in bliss, thinking upon all the vast possibilities. I entered, an insignificant new student, and lined up at the end of a long queue, acutely aware of the looks cast my way. There were plenty of oddities here, but I stood out even more, being that I was half their age.

When I finally stood before the serving line, the cook, the turtle thrower whom I'd met in the kitchen that afternoon, reached down and brought out a dusty bowl, which he wiped with his oily sleeves. He ladled a chunk of yam and two well-simmered taro plants into my bowl and passed it to me.

I thanked him.

Alone in a corner, I ate up my portion, not in elegant bites as Mama would have me do at home, keeping up the rituals of a proud and ancient household, but in hungry horse-munches and noisy slurps. Checking briefly to see that no one was watching, I licked the bottom of my bowl, making sure nothing was wasted, and burped several times in great satisfaction.

Two city boys walked up to my table, looking almost identical, clearly brothers. One, whom I thought of as Young Twin, snatched up the book my father had sent, threatening to throw it away. I snatched it back. What did they want from me? I soon found out. They wanted me to match them up with Sisi and Su Lan. They had fallen in love.

I ignored them, detesting their request. Then came the threat and a flash of a gun hidden under Old Twin's shirt. They knew our family, how rotten it was and why we were here. They had spent fifteen fens, quite a sum, placing a phone call to their aunt, Skinny Ju, Yellow Stone's sole telephone operator. She had told them everything about my family. I froze, then grabbed my bowl and textbook and walked out. They followed me, one on my left side, the other on my right.

Trying to shake them off, I ran toward my sister's room. Sisi and Su Lan were already back, humming some lively revolutionary songs and changing out of their sweaty clothes with the door left ajar. The twins peeped in.

Su Lan rushed out, her fresh shirt hanging open, revealing the budding mounds of her chest and her flat belly. She screamed for the rascals to leave me alone, pushing forcefully with her flimsy hands at their chests. They had no choice but to back away.

16

Routine settled in and normalcy resumed. I found that classes were held at night after a full day of labor. Students were taught by special teachers selected by the commune to replace the regular teachers who had been sent away to work in the fields as part of their reeducation. The substitutes were young farmers from politically powerful families who were barely literate and often had a hard time reading and spelling correctly. This fit the needs of the students here perfectly. Teachers didn't know how to teach and students didn't care about learning.

The only real teacher was Principal Jin, who had been spared reeducation because of the fresh farm produce he sent to the county's education bureau each week.

Sisi said I should not be lazy, so one night after supper I decided to attend the principal's history class. I had just crossed the green flat when the twins suddenly appeared, blocking my path. With smug smiles, they asked me where I was going.

"History class," I answered. I tried to go around them, but they stopped me.

"We want to be your friends, like we said before," Old Twin said. The students called him Lao Yi, which meant Number One Twin. He had a black mole on his right cheek, distinguishing him from Young Twin.

Being friends entailed saying nice things about

them in front of my sister and Su Lan, and having my sister meet them in the grove beyond the hill. When I heatedly refused, Old Twin pulled out his gun and pointed it at the private dining room window, where we could see Sisi and Su Lan engaged in *biǎo zhōng wǔ*, a Communist loyalty dance, with the dinner guests.

Young Twin made lewd comments about my sister, his words sounding so ugly and offensive that I felt blood rush to my head. I smacked Young Twin's face and kneed him in the crotch, taking him by surprise.

Old Twin grabbed me up by the shoulders and tossed me into a muddy puddle.

I screamed and threw chunks of mud at the twins, smearing their faces and clothes. One chunk of mud landed in Young Twin's eye, making him jump up and down and yell in outrage. The two brothers rushed forward and started kicking me. When I screamed louder, they pushed my face down into the puddle so that I was unable to breathe or make a sound, but I kept on fighting, trying to land blows with my elbows and feet. They pressed my head deeper and deeper into the mud. Each time I tried to breathe, mud would enter my nostrils.

My head burst with pain, and I grew weaker and weaker. I felt myself fading and everything became a blur. The next thing I knew, Ya Ba was carrying me into our room and using water from his face basin to scrub the mud from my face, nostrils, and ears while other students gathered around, murmuring in low and concerned voices.

Sisi and Su Lan came a little while later. Sisi was crying, so Su Lan took over washing me. With a hand towel, she gently wiped the corners of my eyes and nose. They thanked Ya Ba, who had returned to his usual quiet state and retreated to his bed.

Sisi kept asking me how I was feeling. I cried

again, a short burst of tears, then smiled and said I was fine. When I recounted what had happened, Sisi didn't scold or lecture me. She borrowed some of Ya Ba's clothes for me to change into. They were two sizes too big, causing the girls to laugh. They fed me a glass of precious sugar water, using Ya Ba's sugar. Happy and contented, Ya Ba offered us some hard candies.

Mrs. Lin and Principal Jin came by later and said that the twins would be punished for almost drowning me. They would be locked up in the janitor's room next to the kitchen for twenty-four hours, with only a night bucket to relieve themselves. They would be able to smell the sweet aroma of cooking dishes but would not have any food.

I asked Principal Jin if he could take their gun away, but the principal shook his head and said it was a problem even the government could not resolve. Guns had been left behind by the Nationalist army when they had fled the mainland. At that time, civilians were encouraged to arm themselves. Now, almost every man owned a gun, women too. They could be bought cheaply and were hidden everywhere, buried in gardens and pigsties.

They thanked Ya Ba and left.

*W*eeks later, April came with layers of mists from the distant sea mingling with dashes of sunlight brighter and steamier than before. Bursts of drizzles—spring storms in the making—were swift overhead like farmers' hands dusting seeds of spring, making the soil soggy and sticky with the nutrients of life. At noon, the sun would make our bodies hot with sweat and unbearable itches. At sundown, it would cool off again with a light rain from the inner mountains, readying for another early morning of foggy mist shrouding our valley.

The months that followed were peaceful. Sisi and I regularly served noon meals for Principal Jin and his dining guests. His guest list had grown to include more local cadres. Twice a week, on Mondays and Thursdays, two green-hatted young Liberation Army soldiers drove an army truck along the uphill dirt road to the school to load the season's harvest of leafy *gai lan*, green onions with giant roots, fat carp leaping in water vats, and piglets. They also loaded sacks of plump white rice, hairy-skinned taros, and long and springy sugarcanes used to make sweet after-meal liqueur drinks. They also hauled away vats of well-simmered, curry-spiced goat meat stew, the cook's specialty, freshly delivered to the county party chief, who would wait patiently for the cook's special offering and whose temper would flair if the stews did not arrive punctually.

Sometimes two trucks came, one for the plants, fruits, rice, and beans we harvested; the other, a noisier truck, to carry the unwilling ducks, geese, mother hens, goats, and pigs, all packed together and secured inside by an iron-latched back door.

Su Lan would help when guests ordered more drinks of wine than I could tend to. The more I poured, the happier they became. The drinking banter always started with talk of politics, but then Principal would say, "Eat. Don't smack empty lips."

They would eat the ten-course fatty meals with rice piled high in their porcelain bowls, smoking in between chewing and biting. Liquor rouged their faces and turned their voices louder. They would unbutton their shirts, loosen a notch or two of their belt buckles, and sink farther back into the woven bamboo armchairs. Even the two young town soldiers did the same, bronzed and trim, though they were at the start of the meals, but the liquor loosened more than buttons on shirts and belt buckles. As we carried dishes back to the kitchen and brought new teapots to the table, the guests would grab Su Lan's hands and her slender waist or plead for Sisi to sit on their laps and help them empty the remaining rice wine from the bottles.

Su Lan always scolded them and slapped away their wrists, as if they were children. Sisi was calmer. She would just ignore them, keeping her eyes on her chores and herself in motion with grace and dignity, though her face would redden whenever she was touched by a stranger's unwanted hands. During those times I'd make myself scarce, not knowing what to do, staying in the kitchen, feeling confused and lost. Principal Jin would look at me with his glazed eyes without offering me any guidance. Instead, there was resignation in his actions: drinking more wine and lighting one more cigarette, as if to shade and shroud himself with smoke and liquor so that what was occurring before him would be unseen.

Mrs. Lin would peep through the seams of the curtain and nudge me back into the rowdy room.

Reluctantly, I would reenter, only to feel shame and anger, and back out again after receiving stares from the dinner guests.

Evening meals, Sisi and Su Lan would serve dinner in Principal Jin's office up the hill. The same lunch guests would return, sometimes with town girls. The meals lasted longer and the singing became louder. You could see the shadows of entwined dancing bodies through the windows, illuminated by a rare fifteen-watt lightbulb.

I would stay up and gaze there from across the campus in my perch with Ya Ba. He would stop staring at the wall and come out to sit by the door with me. He would wait for the girls to come out and then sigh before going back to lie down on his bed. Sisi had told me that Ya Ba had followed Su Lan here. He was in love with her and wanted to marry her. He was not a bad prospect, since he would inherit a hotel business from a rich uncle in Hong Kong.

One night, I was suddenly awoken by Ya Ba after I dozed off to sleep in my cot. He was mumbling, "Useless man, pitiful man," talking to himself as he furiously scraped the bottom of his rice bowl, which was brought to him every day by Mrs. Lin. For the first time, he had eaten it all, every last grain of rice. He stayed up afterward, writing long letters on pages, which he then hid away in his leather trunk.

From that night on, he'd be up all night. When I arose at dawn, I'd find him lying on his wooden bed, snoring as the morning gong sounded.

At night, without anyone to talk to, I would lie in my cot and think of my days at home with Grandpa and Grandma, Mama and Baba, and my siblings, wondering if they were missing me as much as I missed them. Was Baba home from the labor camp yet? Was Mama suffering from her stomach colic? Was Grandpa's cough getting better? Was Grandma's pain easing? What I missed the most was sitting at Grandpa's feet as he napped in the sun, unbothered by his past and untainted by the political sins imposed upon him.

I thought of my friends at school, the classes and the teachers I admired, the joy of learning and of being praised by teachers for my fine calligraphy penmanship and high marks on my homework.

I thought of the hour-long morning run to the elementary school, a former Confucius temple fronted by two soulful lotus ponds with an exquisite arched stone bridge leading to the teachers' offices and small classrooms lining the sides.

In the back of my mind, there was always that bronze school bell tolling far and near our village, signifying the rhythm of life. Often, I dreamed about seeing the skinny teacher hitting the bell and woke up in the middle of the night as if having heard the bell toll, telling me I was late for school and would miss my favorite part of the day: singing the "Long Live Chairman Mao" song.

Deep into the night, snores hummed from the

surrounding barrack rooms like a lullaby. I could hear rice stalks rustle, swaying peacefully and calmly against a gentle breeze, as if the rice fields were dancing in thanks to the earth and sky and moonlight for nourishing them.

In the morning, when the sun was hardly up, Sisi would knock on our door, prompting Ya Ba to uncurl from a fetal position and leap off the bed, a thin blanket around his pale frame.

I would climb off my cot, rubbing my bare feet, left sole over the right one, to warm them from the chilly and damp ground. Ya Ba would glance at Sisi in an unvoiced plea for her to talk to him or step inside an inch. Sisi was Su Lan's best friend. If he could get her to like him, Sisi could be a powerful advocate in bringing Su Lan closer to him. During those awkward long seconds, I would put on my shirt—my only one—and pants, intentionally slowing down my usually quick motions so they could possibly talk.

"Come," Sisi would say from behind the door.

I slipped out the door and could feel Ya Ba following me to lean on the doorframe and open a tiny crack to send me off, watching as we disappeared in the dawn light.

My sister and I would walk up a rise to catch the early light. We'd sit on cool soil as Sisi opened the pages of my textbook, reading each word and passage with me as if she were my language teacher.

"*Xi wang zai lu se de tian yie li*," she read. In the green field lies our hope for the future.

I repeated the words after her, knowing well that her pronunciation was perfect and had been highly regarded by her former teachers. She would correct me if my enunciations were stretched out too high or dragged too low. I repeated them until she gave me a nod of approval.

After the language lesson, she moved on to mathematics. We would add one furrow of rice paddy after another, using the things that surrounded us. She included animals and frogs, numerous around us, as teaching tools. Learning became alive, merged into the parts of nature enveloping us.

When the light became brighter and the sun crept up the horizon to the east, we rushed down the footpath, still dewy from the night's light rain, to embrace a new day.

*O*ne morning after an early meal of rice porridge and yam, Mrs. Lin met Sisi and me at the dining hall entrance with two baskets of fresh yam seedlings at her feet. She wanted us to help her plant the experimental No. 86 yams, just delivered from the county's agriculture nursery. She needed a pair of reliable hands.

We nodded in agreement as she strapped the baskets filled with young plants onto our backs.

The path uphill was dewy, the morning sun weak, not biting yet. The air was sweet, carrying the earth's scent with mixed fruitiness from the trees dotting the crust of the valley. The dense fishy smell of decay back in Yellow Stone was but a memory to me now.

Mrs. Li's footfall was as nimble as that of the green frogs leaping out of our path, frightened at our intrusion. She hummed a lilting mountain tune about a young man courting a beautiful mountain bride from a faraway ridge. She led us up the ridges to a one *mu*—about one-sixth of an acre—half-moon plot with tall bamboos hovering over a dry field.

She said it was shadier and drier, better for the yams, which were supposed to grow twice as big as the usual variety. She asked Sisi if she knew how to plant the seedlings.

Sisi nodded. She was good at planting everything growable under the sun. A farmer's offspring knew her yams. Luckily, she didn't ask me about my farming skills. All I knew about yams was that they tasted fine when fresh, but horrible if they were moldy and half-rotten, which was the only type Mama could afford.

Reassured, Mrs. Lin turned and left, resuming her singing all the way down the hill.

The plowed soil was soft and fluffy, bearing only a thin crust of dampness from the night's frost. There were long rows of furrows with mounded soil in between. The seedlings would be planted on the mounds so that their roots could reach deep and wide, growing fat yams in six weeks.

Sisi dug holes in the raised mounds, and I nestled the roots of the seedlings into each hole. Sometimes the seedlings didn't stay upright and I had to scoop more earth around their base to hold them up. After a row was completed, Sisi would have me stand at the head of the row to run a visual inspection, making sure the seedlings were straight horizontally and upright vertically. She had me pull up the crooked ones, refill the holes, and make them right. Only then would she let me move on to the next row.

It was not even midmorning and my back was already aching from all the bending and kneeling. I quipped that I felt like an old man already. Sisi just smiled, urging me on with the promise of sharing half of her noon dish with me.

A while later, I begged her to let me lie down and rest on the ground for a bit. She nodded, continuing her hole-digging. I took off my shirt and stretched out my limbs like sliced starfruit, feeling the chill of the earth that was slowly warming up. After a few minutes of rest, I was strong again and resumed planting the young yams after her. It was no easy job following her quick hands digging perfect holes, but I was happy spending time with her, having her all to myself instead of sharing her with the rest of the school.

The sun was overhead with the noon meal just around the corner. Dozens of long rows of drab soil mounds were transformed. The rows and columns of leafy young yams all stretched straight and stood upright, judging not just from the head of the plot but from the sides as well.

We scooped up spring water gathered from a knee-high ditch among the nearby bamboo with a wooden bucket, placed there just for this plot in particular, and watered each seedling gently with a ladle of cool water to settle their roots into the new depth.

When the bullhorn sounded from the campus below, calling us to lunch, Sisi and I raced each other back down to the campus flat.

Summer harvest arrived. The terraced fields turned golden with rice plants leaning low to the soil, heavy with the ripening pillowy grain. At first, only the top of the fields was golden, as if lightly painted by the sun, then slowly, as the days passed, the color deepened and the rice stalks themselves yellowed. I could smell the fragrance, unique only to a ripening rice harvest, permeating the gentle land, as if God had spread his generous grace among us.

We would often see Principal Jin bending over the rice stalks to inspect the fullness of the grain by biting on each husk and tasting the ripeness. The fields atop seemed to ripen faster, with their colors turning darker as each rung ascended up the terraced hills. He would plant a bamboo pole into the ground, marking the parcel as ready for harvest the next day. Students would put away all other chores at hand to gather in the chosen fields and cut the golden stalks, furrow by furrow. The harvested stalks were carried down to the thrashing field near the campus flat and stacked up in high piles to shield them from possible storms.

Principal Jin would be among the students, bending and cutting with his sickle, pausing once in a while to smoke a couple of puffs or drink some tea, which Mrs. Lin would have me bring to him. I would work alongside him, gathering what he cut down and laying the stalks in bundles to be bound together into bales the size of mother pigs. Bamboo poles with bladed iron tips at each end were plunged into one bale, then a second bale at the other end, and the pole would be hitched over a shoulder for young students to carry down the hill.

At the end of the day, Principal Jin and I would walk down the hilly footpaths, with him leaning on me at slippery points along the path. He would hum old tunes contentedly as we walked toward a setting sun, returning to the campus flat.

The harvest month of May was bewitching. It brought us dreams of summer, and its woes, as well.

One early morning, the sky was dark and humid, churning with ropey clouds. The temperature dropped so low that my stomach began to ache. I rushed to Sisi's room, crying. Sisi put me in her bed, still cozy with her body heat.

Su Lan fished out a bottle of precious tiger balm, a well-known medicinal concoction for all aches and pains. She squeezed out a fingerful and smeared it over my belly, rubbing it gently, then covering me with Sisi's blanket.

Outside, the crackling noise from a handheld

bullhorn was heard. Principal Jin's announcement was urgent. A severe typhoon was headed this way and the entire school must go to the fields and salvage the season's rice.

Sisi and Su Lan put on extra layers of clothes, topped by a plastic outer sheet given to them to protect them from rain, a modern item that I had never seen before.

Out they rushed.

Ya Ba kicked the girls' door open, holding a bowl of porridge. He placed it on the table and left.

The warm blanket and tiger balm were already helping. I was feeling well enough to gobble down the soupy rice cooked with fermented tofu and roll back into bed again. Outside, the wind had picked up, howling like a demonic creature lurching through the deep valley and mountain peaks.

At noontime the typhoon hit. The guava and banana trees were uprooted, their torn branches flying in the air. The school's lone basketball hoop collapsed, and the shuttered windows in our barracks were thrown open and flapped in and out savagely.

I rushed to the kitchen and saw the cook and Mrs. Lin busily shoveling boiled yams, taros, steamed rice, steamed flour buns, and chunks of simmered pork shoulders into containers for the students' lunch. The kitchen help would carry them up into the hills.

She passed me a bucket containing Principal Jin's lunch and a tin of liquor and told me to take it to him.

Chunky drops of rain began to sluice down. I grabbed up Principal's bamboo bucket and started to leave but was stopped by Mrs. Lin, who ran after me with a few more things she wanted me to bring to Principal Jin—his cigarettes and another coat.

"Stay with him, always, so he doesn't fall," she added.

I nodded and ran up the footpath that was now flattened and made slippery by the rain and the hurrying feet of students returning downhill with heavy, wet bales.

Up the hill, I saw Principal Jin's tall frame. He was standing on a prominent ledge, shouting through his bullhorn. His hand waved a little red flag, guiding throngs of youngsters to different terraces of rice paddies, urging them to cut down as many rice stems as possible and carry them to safety.

When I climbed up the slope, I shouted to the principal and gave him the extra coat. We moved behind a patch of thick pine trees and squatted down. I opened the lid of the bamboo container, revealing his lunch contents. He scooped a bowl for me, filling it with goat stew and rice, then he filled his own portion and shoved big chunks of food into his mouth. Hungrily, I ate, too. The goat meat was legendary. It was the cook's specialty and Principal Jin's favorite dish.

The principal emptied his drink in one gulp.

For the rest of the day, he was the commander in

chief, a roaring old lion shouting orders and giving directions to his students. He rushed to help fallen students, picking up discarded stalks of precious rice and dropped bales. He trekked every footpath to ensure that no plot of the hilly land was neglected and to be sure that all his students were safe.

He slipped a few times, his old linen-stitched sandals broken. He was able to get up again with my help, with me serving as his walking cane. The liquor had gotten the better of him, but he seemed happier and fearless. Even though the wind and rain from the typhoon had ripped apart my rain cover and all his clothes were wet and muddy, he managed to track down the last student up in the most hidden hills and help her carry bales of rice stalks down the slippery, sloshing footpaths.

A bicycle's bell rang—*ding ding ding*—from a distance. The dinging slowly rose from the topographic grades of a hilly path until a bicycle and its rider finally came into view.

In the straight noon sun, biting and prohibitive, a member of the People's Liberation Army in full green uniform materialized on the horizon, riding his bicycle in a gyrating fashion, standing on his pedals to gain each inch of escalation with the front tire nosing this way and that up the dirt road, before finally arriving at the campus flat.

The young officer was a big-eyed, dark-browed political commissar, the type of scribe commonly relied on by the Liberation Army to instill Communist thoughts and Marxist ideals into the hollow minds of new recruits from backward villages. The commissars were the officers who minded the souls of soldiers, not the bullets or bayonets.

Commissar Lai had been newly dispatched from Fujian Military District, Putian Division, to serve as a political advisor at our school, as well as to keep an eye on Principal Jin, they said. When he stepped off his commissioned army bicycle—painted green and marked with a red star—and took off his army hat to wipe the sweat off his pale face with a green army towel, he was instantly surrounded by curious students. We looked him up and down and touched this and that part of his army bicycle and fancy uniform.

As was the custom of this valley, no guest or visitor was officially welcomed until they were greeted by Principal Jin. He came down to the flat to greet the man of politics, not in surprise but in an expectant manner, though most guests were unexpected surprises to us.

Principal Jin and his young visitor barely said anything to each other at first. They didn't even shake hands, as strangers meeting one another would do in this thinly populated mountainous region. It seemed Principal Jin was there only to acknowledge the fact of his arrival and nothing more. That was clear from the way they walked across the flat, two paces apart from each other, the host and his guest. As they walked, they began to talk in low voices.

The encounter was brief.

Later, Mrs. Lin led Commissar Lai to his quarters, a single unit in the same row as our barracks, although detached. It used to serve as a commanding officer's post.

From that day on, one would not just look to

Principal Jin's office atop the hills but also to the detached lair of Commissar Lai to gauge the warmth of the day and chill of the night. An intruder had split the seam of our valley. A storm lay ahead, waiting for us.

*C*ommissar Lai became a constant presence among us, often heard before being seen with his ringing bicycle bell echoing up and down the narrow ridges, orchards, and surrounding cattle farms. Sometimes he would free his hands from the handlebars and let the wheels carry him down the slopes like a carefree eagle until he disappeared, then he would reappear, gyrating up sweatily as we had seen him the very first time when the sound of his ringing bell penetrated the valley. He spent his mornings with male students, cutting rice stalks with sickles, then thrashing them over the sharp nails of the threshing boards. He could be seen climbing tall trees and picking fruits, and tying ropes over mother pigs' necks, readying them for the slaughterhouse.

In quieter times, he walked and talked thoughtfully with older students. In the evenings, he often came to our door, calling on Sisi and Su Lan, both of whom seemed eager and excited to meet the young soldier. I watched them straighten their shirts and check themselves in their shared half-broken mirror before quickly opening the door to receive him. Sisi would blush and Su Lan's eyes would blink even more rapidly. His sudden comings pinged the purity of our school like a pebble falling into a placid pond.

Daily, the three of them—Commissar Lai, Su Lan, and Sisi—would go for long walks around the valley with the soldier and Sisi bookending the blithe Su Lan. From a distance, Ya Ba and I would sit on the raised patch of grass outside our room and watch their long shadows, made longer by a setting light, with the shadow of Su Lan jumping, dancing, and leaping like a ballerina. From the hollow valley, we would hear the abrupt rise of their voices singing or arguing a point, blown to us by an easterly breeze.

One evening we even saw Su Lan being carried on the broad back of Commissar Lai, who later claimed that she had hurt her toes climbing a tree. Another time, Sisi and Commissar Lai carried her like a straight plank, each holding her up under an arm with her laughing all the way down to the campus flat.

Returning to our room, Ya Ba cried and mumbled that Su Lan was his love and that the man was taking her away. He shivered and trembled in his bed and begged me to hold him. I climbed up on his bed and stretched my short arms around his girth from behind. After a while, he started snoring and I returned to my own bed.

The following morning Ya Ba apologized to me for crying like a baby. I wanted to know why it made him sad seeing Su Lan spending time with the

GIRL UNDER A RED MOON

commissar. He said the army man was up to no good and I should be prepared because Sisi would get hurt.

After supper one night, I came to Sisi's room and saw the soldier there again. I asked him if I could join them for the evening walk. The army man said they discussed serious political things for adults and I would not understand any of it.

When they left, Sisi turned and moved her lips, silently mouthing, "Sorry." Su Lan came to peck my cheek before running off with the handsome young soldier.

After I told him about my rejection, Ya Ba surmised that the soldier was going to steal the girls' hearts and ruin their lives. This wisdom came from his own tragic life. A good-looking cadre had seduced his young mother and forced himself on her. His father had killed him and ended up serving a life sentence. The tragic part didn't faze me, but Sisi's heart being stolen would be a problem. As our customs dictated, all my sisters had to be married off in return for a sizable bridal fee. If my sister ran away with a lover for free, then my older brother Jin wouldn't be able to afford a wife and would be forced to live the miserable life of a bachelor.

Ya Ba asked me not to worry about Sisi. She was just being used to make it look fine to the conservative town folk. If they saw a man and woman alone, the locals would hang the man up on a tall tree and beat him to death.

His words only made me worry more. I didn't want anyone to be beaten to death.

He tossed me a little bag of candy—peanut powder sweetened and wrapped in dissolvable rice paper. I swallowed all three bundles in the packs in one bite. It tasted heavenly.

I waited impatiently in my room, trying to read my textbook and do my homework that had been assigned to me by Sisi, but it was no easy task. Ya Ba was no longer quiet. He was agitated, like a wild beast trapped in a cage. He kept on writing long letters to mysterious addresses, which he later asked me to take down to the town's tiny post office. He also started to cook for himself, heating up canned food that was part of the monthly provisions airmailed to him by his rich uncle, the hotel owner.

He even ventured down to the town one day and managed to place a long-distance phone call to a mysterious source. I had come with him, at his request. He asked me to hold his umbrella for him to keep him dry from a midday drizzle. The prize was another package of candies, wonderfully sweet.

On our way back, I asked him whom he had called. He said I didn't need to know. I said he was just like Commissar Lai, brushing me off with the adult-talk lie. He said it was a serious matter and it behooved me to keep my mouth shut. I threw away his umbrella, letting it be blown away by the wet winds, and ran back to the campus.

When he returned to our room, he was drenched.

No matter our agitation and frustration, there was nothing we could do to interrupt Sisi and Su Lan's walks with Commissar Lai. We could only continue the sunset tradition of sitting on the hill and watching the three shadows hovering around the waist of the valley like butterflies.

Ya Ba became more depressed, and I became more worried about Brother Jin's pending bachelorhood. I only knew a few bachelors, including Jin Ju, the principal's brother, and their lives all seemed a misery.

Days came and went, with the sun in the sky getting hotter and cool mountain breezes rarer. Birds stopped flying in the air and hid in the tree foliage, absently singing their monotonous broken tunes alongside loud and spirited cicadas, who glued their bodies to the rough bark of trees.

Sisi and Su Lan's sojourns continued, though the

tenor of their excursions seemed to have changed. The three shadows were less animated. Su Lan made fewer leaps and jumps, and her laughter was lower and less frequent. There were no more piggyback rides for Su Lan on Commissar Lai's back. Neither was there loud singing or chasing among the three of them along the narrow margins of the terraced fields.

Sullenness seemed to have crept into their ritual and their daily lives. There were sheets of printed paper they carried back to their room, new leaflets delivered by the army trucks on their biweekly food scavenger trip from Putian, where the Communist leaders reigned. Su Lan and Sisi read them, word by word, testing the newest catchphrases delivered from the high throne of power, such as *three criticisms*, *anti-feudalism*, *anti-Confucianism*, and *anti–four olds*. They would take longer walks up the hill, staying until the valley was wrapped seamlessly by darkness.

A short while later, Principal Jin's history class was canceled. When I asked Sisi why, she told me sadly that the principal would be condemned soon.

"Why?" I asked.

"For his bourgeois lifestyle," she said.

Every morning, I saw Principal Jin pacing the front yard of his hilltop office like a tamed lion. I heard the students murmuring; they said he was being investigated by the young commissar. His back seemed more bent, burdened by the invisible things he carried. Sometimes I saw him walk with Commissar Lai on the campus flat, having the kind of talk that was brooding, uneasy, and heavy, the kind that separated men from men and beasts from beasts.

There were fewer lunches that I served for

Principal Jin and his guests. Most of the time now, he ate the meals I delivered alone. He would offer me the leftovers, which I would eat later in my room, and I would collect his empty bowls and plates and bring them back to the cook, who would ask me how the old man liked the food he had prepared for him.

Now forbidden to leave his office, the principal spent long hours smoking and drinking the tea I brewed, and writing thoughtfully and lengthily at his desk, with his calligraphy brush sweeping over long scrolls of coarse rice paper. I would help by pulling straight the ends of the scrolls, making the paper lay flat and smooth so the black rice ink wouldn't bleed.

He was a good calligrapher, but Grandpa was better.

I never told him so.

One noonday, the local town mayor arrived with his usual retinue of militiamen, many of them former bandits like himself. The mayor wore his former bandit attire: a pistol stuffed into a big-buckled old belt, black jacket and black trousers with the leg bottoms tied around his ankles, a pair of grass-bladed sandals, and a headband with the label of *wandering soldiers* written on the front.

When Commissar Lai ran urgently to meet the local men at the entrance, the other students and I followed him. He passed a handwritten note to the visiting mayor, but the burly old bandit ignored him altogether. The mayor and his men pushed the soft-skinned city soldier aside, but Commissar Lai caught up and grabbed the mayor's shoulder, stopping him from taking another step. The frustrated mayor turned and spat in his face.

Wiping the spit off his face, Commissar Lai pulled out his pistol and fired a shot into the air, shouting that he would kill them if the town mayor didn't leave.

We all ran for cover, some students hiding behind tree trunks, others dropping down on the ground.

The two men pointed guns at each other.

A shootout would have ensued were it not for the timely appearance of Principal Jin on the hill outside his office. He shouted for the men to stop, flapping his long hands, and told the mayor to leave.

After a long lull, the mayor bowed to Principal Jin and left with his men.

24

I was wrenched from my dream by a sharp whistle blown in the quiet air. Principal Jin's bullhorn crackled, but it was Commissar Lai's voice we heard. "Wake up, all students. Let us condemn the corrupt Principal Jin." The commissar's voice was firm and dark.

Ya Ba leaped out of his bed like a carp and shook my shoulders, but I was already awake. My heart tightened with old fear. The curse of the Revolution was following us. The vast earth had run out of places for us to hide.

The bullhorn crackled again. All farm work was canceled. Revolution took priority.

On the campus flat was a new stage, built overnight with freshly felled pine lumber. A black cloth banner ran the width of the stage, hanging between two leaning trees. White paper slogans were pasted on the banner, announcing a public criticism of Principal Jin. The outer walls of the dining hall were plastered, too, with paper slogans bearing ugly but familiar words—*anti-communism*; *counterrevolution*; *stinking, rotten principal*; *feudal revisionism*; and *corruptors of young minds*. They were accompanied by students' ant-like writings accusing our principal of this or that false crime.

Crowds floated like sludge toward the stage. Sisi and her friend floated with them. Su Lan wasn't giggling or laughing as she often did. Neither was my sister. There was heaviness in their stride, and sadness at their hearts. Other students were delighted at having this day off, a relief from the drudgery of farm work, joking and teasing among themselves, but not my sister, her friend, Ya Ba, and me.

At the opposite end of the campus flat, the twins led a pack of other students, all wearing new green army uniforms with red armbands over their sleeves and army hats, to which shiny medallion images of Chairman Mao were pinned. A newly formed Criticism Brigade marched toward the center of the gathering, shouting slogans. When they arrived in front of the stage, the brigade saluted Commissar Lai, who was standing loftily on the stage, one hand holding the bullhorn and the other waving his pistol. He gestured for the twins, his new right-hand men, to join him on the stage and dismissed the rest, who scattered among the audience. It was no surprise that the twins had sided with Commissar Lai against Principal Jin, who had punished them many times.

Seeing the four of us approaching, the twins leaped down from the shaky stage and ordered us to sit closest to the stage, in the front row. Ya Ba was sent to the second row.

The corners of Sisi's mouth sagged, her eyes downcast. The tails of her vivid eyebrows drooped like limp leaves weighted down by raindrops. Su Lan looked despondent. Her big bright eyes were dimmed with dullness, no longer rapidly blinking. They hardly moved as she stared into emptiness.

On the stage, Commissar Lai surveyed his battlefield, deliberately ignoring Sisi and Su Lan, his designated protégés no longer. His aloof eyes swept the vast, restless crowd.

He nodded to the twins, and his deputies rushed our principal out of his office and down the steps, his old feet barely able to keep up with the quick pace. His long arms were tied behind his back, his wrists fastened by roughly knotted rope. A big wooden board with the words *Fǎn Gé Mìng*—counterrevolutionary element—hung from his neck, bowing down his neck and back with its weight.

Sisi dared only look at him from the corners of her eyes as he was pushed past. Su Lan stared stoically at the stage, as if the scenes of cruelty were unreal and illusory. My heart ached deep inside me like an ulcer. I had seen my own baba hung by both thumbs from the ceiling at the hands of our commune's cadres. This cut me deeply.

In the forcibly maddened dash up the shaky steps to the stage, the principal's slow feet caught the edge of an upturned pine plank, and he fell on his broad face with a thud that was heard across the quiet. Some students gasped, others cried. The twin brothers didn't bother helping him up. They stomped their feet on the man's back and neck and white-haired skull, then grabbed a fist of his hair and pulled him up. The principal's legs were trembling and his nose was broken, with blood oozing from his broken bridge and gashed lips that had been cut by his own teeth. The brothers dragged him without concern to the center of the stage and forced him down onto his knees. The condemned man waiting for his guillotine.

With disgust, the young commissar looked down on the pitiful old principal. He ordered the twins to collect the empty liquor bottles that had been placed on the stage, then proceeded to smash each of the used wares slowly, creating a thick patchwork of glass shards. Coming to stand face-to-face with his nemesis, the commissar squatted down before the principal and slowly unfastened his belt. He removed Principal Jin's shoes and pulled off his pants, leaving him clad only in baggy boxer shorts.

The commissar ordered Principal Jin to confess all the crimes he had committed against the cause of the Revolution, but the man shook his head. He spoke but said nothing that the commissar wanted to hear. When Principal Jin mentioned the certificates of achievements given him by the Education Ministry, praising his dedication and his diligence to the Party, the commissar angrily elbowed the twins. They picked up the principal by his arms and thrust him down to kneel on the broken glass. The principal winced but did not cry out or plead. Gritting his teeth, he settled his lumbering weight on the glass cutting into his flesh.

Su Lan was the first condemner. Like a shadow of her former self, Su Lan gingerly walked up the steps to the center of the stage next to the principal. She looked to the commissar, who nodded back approvingly. She began to read in a thin voice that was not her own, accusing him of raping her on a distant day when she was asked to rub the principal's back after he had fallen in the field. She had been left alone with the principal and he had undressed her and forced himself on her.

I knew that to be a blatant lie, just like the false accusations they had imposed on my father and my grandfather.

The accused kept his eyes on his accuser. The accuser looked away, avoiding the indignation in his eyes. He shook his head as she told her story with sobs and tears. Su Lan abruptly swung her arm, slapping the principal's face. The principal swayed and nearly fell from the blow, but he recovered. Again, she swung her arm. This time her fist caught the side of his head. His body swung with the impact, making his knees dig even harder into the cutting shards. He yielded his first little cry of pain while glaring at Su Lan as if she were a wanton child and nothing more.

"She's lying!" roared Mrs. Lin as she ran up to the stage, waving both arms. "She is lying!"

The twins jumped on Mrs. Lin. Bending her arms backward, they forced her up onto the stage to kneel next to the principal. But she was not to be easily subdued. She shouted to the audience of the injustice being done to her. She was the daughter of a Red Army platoon leader who had fought with the Communists, driving away their enemy and helping build the new republic, and the country owed her a debt that should not be paid back this way. Old Twin produced a pair of blunt scissors and started chopping her hair wildly while Young Twin held down her flailing arms. Before long, her long silky hair was gone, revealing her pale and white skull in rough patches, reducing her from an elegant lily flower to a tiny frail woman. She stopped struggling and just stared at the sheared chunks of her hair at her feet.

It was Sisi's turn next to speak against the principal. I did not think she would lie like Su Lan had. She was always that way, honest, modest, and blunt-spoken. What would she say, lies or truth? I could not say. Things around us had changed. Su Lan had. Would Sisi?

Sisi hesitated, stood up, and slowly walked up onto the stage, her eyes downcast, holding a piece of paper, her written confessions. She stood next to Su Lan and talked about her encounter with Jin Ju, Principal Jin's brother, and how kind he was, sending her to this school. She said we only paid a portion of the tuition and could not afford to give the principal a bribe. She sobbed deeply, her young body shaking uncontrollably, as if the morning air had suddenly turned into a freezing rain. I burst into tears and climbed up onto the stage, crying, "Big sister, let's go home," and rushed into her trembling arms. We held each other tightly.

"Let's go back," I begged.

She just nodded.

"Your sister chooses to stand with the enemy. You are our enemy now," I heard the commissar say.

It all became a blur. All I heard was shouts and cries around me.

Long live the Cultural Revolution!

25

When the drama ended, the twins told us that we were to be detained up in the principal's office, where we could reflect and volunteer our confessions.

Mrs. Lin, Sisi, and I helped the wounded principal walk up the hilly steps, with Sisi and me supporting him on either side and Mrs. Lin gently pushing his back. He winced at each step, his raw knees dripping with scarlet blood.

The twins locked us inside the office.

As soon as the twins were gone, Sisi untied the

rope fastening Principal Jin's arms. Once freed, he sighed and sat down on the dirt floor as we surrounded him and began to take out bits of glass that had embedded in his kneecaps and cleaned the blood off his face, neck, and sunken thighs. We laid him down on his side like a wounded beast, and he said nothing except to gesture at me to get a cigarette lit for him.

I did and he gave me a nod.

At midnight, I climbed out the rear window and snuck through the back door of the kitchen. Under the sink, I found a large pot the cook had hidden for us, filled with leftover pork belly taro stew that was minced with the spices the principal loved. I carried it stealthily back to our temporary jail and passed it through the window to my sister, who waited nervously.

We ate silently but hurriedly, then I climbed out again, carrying the emptied pot back to the kitchen. I took a hidden bottle of rice wine from a hole in the wall, a secret hiding place in the kitchen, and returned with it to Principal Jin. This time he smiled.

He shared the wine with Mrs. Lin.

Mrs. Lin even offered a sip to Sisi, but she demurred and busied herself with her task of dressing the wounds on the principal's mangled knees. The night was long and the air cool. The wolf dogs were howling and some other creatures, too.

In time, I fell asleep, lying on the floor next to Sisi, in her embrace. In the other corner, the principal lay curled up in a fetal position facing the wall. Mrs. Lin sat, leaning against a wall corner, vigilant.

At daybreak, the twins unlocked the office, stormed inside, and took the principal out. I peeped through a window and watched as they dragged him down to the milking station on the campus flat. Dropping the principal, they threw a staunch rope over the main beam of the bamboo roof. Principal Jin barely opened his eyes, letting the young students do their damnedest to his wounded body. They bound his wrists in front of him, tied one end of the rope around his wrists, and heaved him up. The principal's limp body was jerked and straightened like a dormant puppet being stirred alive by his puppeteer as they raised him higher and higher until he dangled with only his toes barely touching the ground. He was left hanging there as they shouted for him, once again, to reflect and confess, and sauntered off, a pair of thugs proud of their folly.

Some students came by to silently stare at us, as if we were odd animals kept in isolation, but there was not much to see and they soon went back down to watch the spectacle that was their principal being condemned—only daring to look at him from a distance. They shouted no condemnations at him nor uttered any sneering words. In time, they strolled away and headed up to their terraced fields to till their soil, plant their vegetables, and spread their seeds as if life was the same as it had been yesterday.

Three times I watched as the twins came by to beat Principal Jin with the butts of their rifles, hitting and slamming him all over his body. The brute force of their blows made him swing from left to right and twirl around. After a time, the twins would grow tired and saunter off.

At noontime, it was Sisi's turn.

Commissar Lai came to the hilltop office. He was sullen, not smiling or full of laughter like before when he had just been a young soldier from a big city with a green army bicycle. Now he was a man of politics, a man of mighty weight and authority. He moved slower now, with less buoyancy.

He sat before Sisi as she squatted in a corner whimpering and tried to sway her to give false testimony against Principal Jin.

Again and again, she shook her head, refusing to say anything.

"I'll make a long-distance telephone call to Yellow Stone Communist Public Security Office," he threatened. "They will come and arrest you immediately."

Anger and fear choked my throat. I wanted to jump at this man and smash the wooden stool I sat on over his head, hurting him the way he had hurt the principal and Mrs. Lin. I wanted to make him go away forever so my sister and I didn't have to live in fear of being captured and put in jail for crimes we didn't commit and words we didn't say.

Mrs. Lin shook her head, warning me.

As Commissar Lai rose in disappointment, Mrs. Lin begged him to let the principal down, but the army man ignored her, holding his arrogant chin high.

Kicking open the door, he left.

When the twins carried Principal Jin back to the office, he was delirious. He was badly burned by the sun, and his legs and arms were raw and bloody with new wounds. They dumped him on the floor and left.

Sisi carefully cleaned the new wounds. The principal's face was bruised and swollen, his lips bloody where the twins had slapped him again and again after failing to coerce any confessions from him.

When the evening air was quiet and cool, I climbed out again and fetched some tea for the principal, but he couldn't even keep tea down, vomiting out all that we fed him. Principal lay weakly on the cold floor.

When the stars shone in the night sky, Mrs. Lin left without a word, climbing out the window and disappearing into the forest. She returned several hours later with four local young men, who climbed through the window and hauled the weak principal out the window. They carried him away on a bamboo stretcher they lifted over their shoulders. Their footfalls were light in the night air and darkness shrouded them with secrecy.

Mrs. Lin stayed with us, even though she could have left this hellhole. She said she wanted to take the blame. She didn't want us to suffer anymore.

The twins came the next morning and saw that Principal Jin was gone. They left without a word, after casting angry glances at us. In the campus flat, they were met by Commissar Lai. There was intense talking and angry gesturing. The commissar slapped the twin brothers and walked away, leaving them stunned and shamed.

They came back up to unlock the office door, and Sisi and I were free to return to the barracks. When we arrived at Sisi's room, the door was locked. It was usually left ajar. Sisi knocked on the door.

When the door finally opened, it was as if by silent mice and not by Su Lan's unseen hand.

Back at my room, Ya Ba greeted me with a huge grin. He took me into his arms and squeezed me with a tight hug, whispering that Sisi was his heroine, and I his little hero.

The next few days showed an obvious strain between Sisi and Su Lan. Their close relationship seemed shattered by the lie told by one and the truth told by the other.

Ya Ba and I decided to intervene. We went to their room one evening after supper. Ya Ba nudged me and I pulled the girls' hands together so that they were clasped. No words were exchanged, but I sensed that the thawing of their tension had begun.

28

Ya Ba woke me up the following morning. He was crying and clutching his face between his hands. I sat up in my bed, wanting to know why he was upset. He said that Commissar Lai had taken Su Lan to his room for further questioning and had assaulted Su Lan, leaving her with torn and bloodied clothing.

I rushed to Sisi's room to find her door shut and latched. I pasted my ear to the thin door, trying to catch any sound uttered or word spoken. There was only Su Lan's faint sobs and shallow crying, and

Sisi's, as well, their voices mixing together. Scared, I returned to my room and crept back into my bed, my heart heavy with worry.

Ya Ba spent the night fumbling over his things, locking and unlocking his suitcases. Then he left our room. Hours later, he returned, silent as usual.

29

The day broke with the sound of the noisy bull-horn blaring in the morning air as the twins, fighting over the horn, tried to make some announcement as part of their new responsibilities.

Students milled about the campus flat aimlessly at breakfast time. The old order was gone, and things seemed to have gone awry. No smoke rose from the chimneys of the kitchen. Students wandered around the empty dining hall, hungry and angry.

Ya Ba said the cook had left. He took out some canned food. It was really good meat. I had two cans of it, he had three. It was divine. We burped loudly.

When I met Sisi in the campus flat, I asked her when we could go home, even though what I was burning to know was the meaning of Su Lan's bloodstains. She asked me to wait and said that things were changing for the better. I said that things were hardly better. Principal Jin was carried away, leaving us to fend for ourselves, and the cook had followed him, leaving us nothing to eat. And there was the news about Su Lan's bloodstains and the frightening word *assault*. It's nothing, Sisi said. She was caring for her, and Su Lan was already much better.

I knew she downplayed the significance of the incident so I would not worry, but the inkiness of that blood lingered long in my mind.

By sundown, talk of Commissar Lai's disappearance had spread throughout the school. The twins were despondent and looked lost. They sat at their table in the dining hall, not talking or eating the food that Mrs. Lin had taken over cooking—rice, yam, taro, and some goat meat.

That evening we were asked to gather in the dining hall, long past our regular bedtime, huddling together in the weak lighting of a fifteen-watt electric bulb that flickered in the cool breeze. The town mayor had come to make an announcement.

He stood on one of the tables. The first thing he said stunned us. They had found Commissar Lai's bicycle on a mountain cliff, but not the commissar himself. The Bridge Town Communist Committee had already reported his disappearance as a suicide. The mayor said he would be in charge of running the school until a new principal was assigned and the school would return to its old ways, set up by Principal Jin.

No one asked any questions about the commissar, but we all clamored to know where our old principal had gone. The mayor claimed to know nothing about Principal Jin's whereabouts and jumped off the table, heading to the private dining room in the back.

On the day we left the school, we went to say goodbye to Mrs. Lin. She took us to the plot where the No. 86 experimental yams were planted. She dug a hoe into a mound and revealed a bunch of ripened yams, each a foot long and as plump as a baby.

It was the first time I had seen such big, beautiful yams, and something that had come from my own labor. Sisi and I laughed, overjoyed and overwhelmed by the grace of this land and the abundance it gifted us. Mrs. Lin bagged the yams for us to take home.

We didn't have to walk all the way home this time. Ya Ba had arranged to have a three-wheeled motor-cycle fetch him and Su Lan to return to Jian Kou, their hometown. He invited Sisi and me to ride with them until the dirt country road came to a fork. One bend led to their fancy seaside town with rich families from Hong Kong and big houses built with capitalist money. The other led farther north to Yellow Stone.

Sisi and Su Lan didn't talk much but held hands all the way like sisters, until they parted tearfully.

Ya Ba smoked filtered cigarettes all the way, whistling some revolutionary tunes, not a care in his heart. The old talk of Su Lan's loss of purity and the possible ruination of her future seemed to have evaporated as soon as Bridge Town was out of our sight. After parting with us, they vanished into the vast landscape, leaving behind only a storm of dust.

Sisi and I slung our belongings over our shoulders, and we walked for another hour to our village.

We arrived at home in the darkness of night.

Mama and my siblings were all excited to see us and hugged us in quiet embraces. We talked and laughed, which awoke Grandma and Grandpa. We rushed into their room and jumped on their big bamboo bed, relishing the joy of being together again.

Life in Yellow Stone pushed forward like waves in the sea as we awaited another purge, another episode of craziness, another oddly named movement to wash onto our shore. And come again it would, in cycle after continuous cycle, as long as Chairman Mao kept on breathing, old and feeble though he had become. Mao had grown up a young revolutionary, zestfully trying to liberate our suffering nation from famine, corruption, warlords, and endless wars. In the end, however, he had become a ruthless and bitter emperor, letting his own desires rule his mind and darken his soul. But for now, Cult-Rev had receded like an ebbing tide, fading as quickly as it had come upon Yellow Stone.

The fire from the initial sparks had vanished by the time Sisi and I returned home from Bridge Town. The paper slogans pasted on the street archways, temple columns, and our commune's announcement boards had been washed away by the wet rains of spring. Scraps of propaganda posters and paper flags carrying words like *Mao* and *culture* were scattered everywhere like lost souls, waiting to be picked up by the town's street sweeper, a finely dressed old lady named An Nei.

An Nei didn't seem to mind the dirt and mud. She had flowers in her hair and wore a silk jacket with matching pants, their wide bottoms riding above her ankles. Delicate silk laces were tied around her ankles and fluttered in time to her sweeping. Villagers said she dressed so delicately for her absent husband, who had been rotting away in jail the last twenty years for embezzlement. It was said she had been permitted to visit her man once and had taken the whole month off to journey to An Xi, a city hidden in the mountains. She had no children and no house, living in one tiny room at the windy end of town.

An Nei was the same, but other changes had taken place. There was a rumor that our commune's gun-toting party chief would soon be on his way out of his cushy position, after being caught having an affair with a barefoot nurse who cared for farmers in the muddy fields and was the wife of a powerful political leader who headed another minor faction within the Communist Party. Some said he had been framed; the other faction wanted him out and the only way to hasten his downfall was through corruption charges.

At Sisi's school, we heard that Mr. Ma, her former political studies teacher, had been transferred away due to ailing parents, whom he had to care for. That wasn't the only change. The school principal had been suddenly reduced to the rank of an average teacher, teaching math—something to do with his private feud with the commune's party chief. The principal had once written a complaint to Putian

County's education bureau, accusing the party chief of stealing textbook money allocated to Yellow Stone Middle School.

Each time the former principal passed our house along the street in the afternoon, he walked on the opposite side of the road, as far away from our door as possible. It could be that he was ashamed of having ruined the life of a young girl, or maybe he just liked to walk on the shady side of the street as the sun set in the horizon. Which one it was, I would never know. All that mattered was the cursed Revolution was waning like a weak moon. No one was shouting any crazy slogans; peace had descended once again on our ancient village.

Dr. Tang, the accordion-playing English teacher, came by our house one day to tell us about his transfer to Putian County's No. 1 Middle School, a very prestigious post. He was being promoted because his father, an old cadre belonging to the New Faction within the Party, was in favor now, which meant Dr. Tang's reeducation time was over.

He talked with Sisi, sympathy in his tone and on his face as he asked about her work in the fields. When he asked if Sisi still sang, she nodded, and he said that maybe, someday in the future, he could invite her to choreograph for the young dancers in his new school, the top middle school in the county. Sisi blushed, her face burning red like a lychee.

When he left, a heavy bag on his right shoulder and the accordion over his left shoulder, he walked on the sunny side of the street. Sunlight shone down on his instrument, making it gleam. It was as if a halo wreathed him.

32

One glorious June morning, Sisi asked me to go in her stead to pay a visit to her savior, Jin Ju.

Hearing my footsteps, he crawled out of his rickety hut put together with planks, bamboo leaves, half a doorframe, and some broken window glass, and greeted me cheerfully. He was golden, shiny and smooth-skinned, well baked by the unrelenting sun.

I passed Jin Ju a bottle of rice wine that Mrs. Lin had wanted me to bring him. The shepherd twisted off the lid and gulped down a mouthful. His face broke into knobs of painful delight.

I asked him about his brother, the principal, whom I worried about and thought of even in my dreams. He said not to worry. Bridge Town folks always took care of good outsiders. His brother was the best outsider to have come their way.

I knelt down on the soil, thanking him for the good news.

EPILOGUE

*S*isi never went back to school; it would have been tempting a tiger's wrath. She never even ventured near the school. In the town of Yellow Stone, she was forgotten, as were many used and discarded creatures, but the land of Yellow Stone remembered her. Mountains and rivers embraced her. She signed up as a full member of Yellow Stone Commune's Fifth Production Brigade, officially a farmer now.

Every day she rose with the sun, carrying a hoe, a sickle, or a pair of wooden buckets, and headed out to the green, muddy fields of her future. Every night she climbed into the bed shared with her sisters, after cooking the evening meal for the family and feeding our ailing grandma with a big spoon.

"You're a woman now," I heard Grandma say to Sisi between bites of soft tofu and sweet yam. "You'll marry a good man. Life will go on just fine."

Sisi blushed shyly at hearing those words and fed Grandma another spoonful of soft food.

The day Sisi turned twenty-six—an advanced age beyond marriage—our village matchmaker brought three young men to our house, seeking my sister's hand in marriage.

The first man left before even taking his shoes off, as the customs required, muttering, "Stinking landlord's family. I should have known. Who wants to marry a blemished woman from a stained family?"

The second man took off his shoes and entered, only to retreat after stepping on some chicken poop.

"Condemned and poor," he said, and rushed out our door without a word of polite courtesy.

The third one came late. He talked quietly, politely, and with great interest with Baba, who had been temporarily released from his labor reform camp. They had a brief yet warm chat before the matchmaker flocked Sisi and the young man into our back room, which overlooked the river.

When the sun began to set and the seabirds swirled in the air, looking for their nightly nests, there was still no sign of the young man and Sisi from behind the closed door.

At suppertime, Sisi finally came out, her face reddened.

Mama asked what was taking so long. The day was ending and he had to walk for hours back to his home.

Sisi said he was asking for permission to spend the night here and was fine with sharing the bed with her little brother, me.

Sisi looked at me, and I nodded.

Mama asked which one he was.

"The forest worker from Hanjiang," Baba answered, taking a deep draw from Grandpa's water pipe.

"Oh," said Mama, "the tall one with big eyes."

That evening meal, at our humble table, became Sisi's engagement dinner, shared quietly but joyfully by the entire family.

A month later, they were married in the simplest wedding ceremony of my memory. No big banquet, no villagers invited, just family and cousins.

The following day they packed her things, and we walked with them to the bus station, from which they would take a long-distance bus ride to Lian Cheng, a mountainous town where his company was located deep inside the Fujian mountains. Sisi wore a red blouse and a pair of black silk shoes Mama had stitched for her for the special occasion. I gave her a small basket filled with the No. 86 yam seedlings that I knew would grow big and plump in the mountainous soil.

The newlyweds held hands as they walked, with Sisi leaning on his shoulder, and his arm holding her close. Ahead of us, the land stretched long and wide, making them look like tiny seedlings in spring. There would be full rains and sunlight aplenty in summer and fall. There would even be winter's frost and bone-chilling wind blown into their path, but they were one now, and forever shielded by a God that is good and merciful.

CHINA'S CULTURAL REVOLUTION BEGAN IN THE SUMMER OF 1966, AS MAO ZEDONG, LEADER OF THE CHINESE COMMUNIST PARTY, CALLED ON THE COUNTRY'S YOUTH TO REJECT BOURGEOIS VALUES AND "IMPURE" ELEMENTS OF SOCIETY. MAO, WHO FELT THAT THE GOVERNMENT AT THAT TIME WAS LEADING CHINA IN THE WRONG DIRECTION, SHUT DOWN SCHOOLS, URGING STUDENTS TO EMBRACE A REVOLUTIONARY SPIRIT. THE MOVEMENT GAINED MOMENTUM AS STUDENTS THROUGHOUT THE COUNTRY ORGANIZED INTO PARAMILITARY GROUPS CALLED THE RED GUARD, WHICH CONDEMNED OLDER CITIZENS, LANDOWNERS, AS WELL AS CHINA'S INTELLIGENTSIA—SUBJECTING MANY TO HARASSMENT, BEATINGS, AND OTHER DISPLAYS OF PUBLIC CASTIGATION—AND FOUGHT AGAINST THE "FOUR OLDS" OF CHINESE SOCIETY: OLD CUSTOMS, OLD CULTURE, OLD HABITS, AND OLD IDEAS.

BELOW, THE PHOTOGRAPH SHOWS A GROUP OF YOUNG RED GUARD MEMBERS HOLDING THE RED BOOK OF MAO'S QUOTATIONS AND WEARING THE ICONIC RED ARMBANDS.

做人要做这样的人

将革命进行到底

A PROPAGANDA POSTER URGING YOUNG PEOPLE TO JOIN THE REVOLUTION SHOWS A MEMBER OF THE RED GUARD HOLDING THE RED BOOK.

A PRODUCTION BRIGADE OF PEASANT FARMERS WORKS IN A FIELD IN 1967 CHINA, WITH A BLACKBOARD IN THE FOREGROUND BEARING QUOTATIONS FROM CHAIRMAN MAO.

MEMBERS OF THE RED GUARD PUT ON A STREET THEATER PRODUCTION DISPLAYING REVOLUTIONARY THEMES AND A PORTRAIT OF CHAIRMAN MAO, IN MAY 1967 SHANGHAI.

ACKNOWLEDGMENTS

I thank our creator for all the good things in life.

I thank Joseph Reynolds, a phenomenal writer, for helping transform my handwritten pages into finely typed text. My sincerest thanks also to his fellow writer, Amber Smith, who labored hard over this project.

Sunny, my dear wife, is my rock and my life. Once again, she has worked her magic in helping polish this book. *Love* is a weak word for what I feel for her. Victoria and Michael, my love for you both graces every word I write, as deep and thick as the blood we share.

I'm indebted to my sister, Sisi, for being who she is to me—a precious, motherly big sister who always took care of me.

I am in awe of Lisa Sandell, the most thoughtful and brilliant editor, a celebrated author and poetess herself, truly a writer's best friend because she understands and loves us. I feel as if we swim in the same river of poetry, each poetic word our oar.

To my ablest agent, Alex Glass, you are my wisest guidance. I am honored to have you on my side.

My gratitude to Elliot Figman, executive director of Poets & Writers, who has kindly mentored me since my early days as a naïve writer.

To my friend Albert Litewka for your caring brotherly love.

For my dear cousins, Shih-Ho and Feng-I Chen, and Shih-Yueh and Kuo-Hua Chang, you are my truly loving family.

My humblest gratitude to Bill and Laurie Benenson, two fellow artists with the biggest hearts and kindest souls.

To my mother-in-law, Alice Liu, and my extended family, Nate and Kui, I love you guys so much.

ABOUT THE AUTHOR

DA CHEN'S life is a true immigrant success story. A native of China, Da grew up in a tiny village without electricity or running water. He was a victim of Communist political persecution and harrowing poverty during the Cultural Revolution, but his dreams enabled him to soar above these hardships. He excelled while studying at the Beijing Language and Culture University, and remained there as a professor of English after graduating at the top of his class. Da arrived in America at the age of twenty-three with only thirty dollars and a bamboo flute. He went on to attend the Columbia University School of Law on a full scholarship and to write several books.

Da is the *New York Times* bestselling author of *Colors of the Mountain*, a memoir; its sequel, *Sounds of the River*; the middle-grade novel *Wandering Warrior*; and *Brothers*, among several other titles. He lives in Southern California with his family.